The Revelare: Truths Hidden In Plain Sight

Thelma,
Thank you fa bein thu my day. A hope this book is a blessin to yo —

[signature]

The Revelare

Paul K. Lott, Sr.

The

Revelare

Truths Hidden In Plain Sight

Paul K. Lott, Sr.

The Revelare

ISBN 978-1-943277-58-2

Printed in USA by Revelare Press

Dedication

I dedicate this book to my wife, Crystal, for all her love and support. If there is any thing in my life that shows me how much the Heavenly Father cares for me, its that He brought me a miracle in the form of my wife. I also want to thank my children for loving me and teaching me to be a better man through parenting.

The Revelare

Paul K. Lott, Sr.

Table of Contents

The Revelare

Praefatio

I find that most people have a grade school understanding of the Bible and what it teaches. As young children, many of us attended some kind of Sunday school to learn the basics. Most religious education comes to a sudden stop after grade school. By the time we are teens, we no longer have an interest in going to church. For the rest of our lives, we look at religion and God through the eyes of a child. Most of what is handed down through our pastors is essentially an expanded version of our grade school Bible education.

Most people don't read the Bible even when they read the Bible. For example, most people think the Bible teaches that God created the universe in the Book of Genesis when, in fact, the Bible contains no account of the creation of the universe. Most people think that God created the planet Earth in the Genesis account of the creation, when, in fact, the Earth already existed when the story begins and the Bible tells us that it already existed. Every time I make this claim, my minister and lay friends object and demand that I prove it, so here is the proof.

The Bible starts with these words: "In the beginning God created the Heavens and the Earth." After I read the first line, my friends usually say, "See, you are wrong!"

But then there is the second line: "Now the Earth was formless and empty, darkness was over the surface of the deep, and the Spirit of God was hovering over the waters." The second sentence opens with the words; "Now the Earth was . . ." The Earth was already here. It was in a disorganized condition, but it already existed. The passage talks about there being darkness over the surface, it mentions water, and tells us that God was hovering over this water. The Bible does not use the word "create" as in "create from nothing." The Bible uses the word create in the same way we would say that someone created a new work of art, or created a new model of car. In both cases, creation is using existing raw materials to create something useful.

This is a simple example, but an important one, because it demonstrates how our thinking influences what we think we are reading. The Bible is filled with truths hidden in plain sight because people are reading it through the fog of their past learning. The Revelare is designed to clear the fog because the fog leads most people to believe doctrines and live lives that don't lead to their eventual goal of an afterlife in Heaven. The Revelare will not only clear away the fog of false beliefs and practices, but will clarify the principles that lead to a better life and an eventual place in Heaven.

Most of what I have written here, I have taught in small circles for years. At first, I did not write this book because many of the ideas felt incomplete. It turns out that I needed more experience in life to grasp what some of the passages were trying to teach me. Until I gained the right experiences, I struggled to write the words.

For the past few years, I was simply lacking in courage. I have done a lot of work in and out of the mainstream church community. The mainstream Christian community holds to some pretty wrong ideas about God and the purpose of the Christian life. These ideas have led a lot of people to abandon the formal church community, and classify themselves as "spiritual but not religious." How does one address the doctrinal challenges of the mainstream churches in a way that does not alienate them? How does one remain a vital part of the church community after telling that community that many of its core beliefs are false and have no place in the Bible they claim as their authority? In the end, it comes down to courage.

I believe that *The Revelare: Truths Hidden In Plain Sight* is an important book that can open up a life of faith to multitudes that struggle to find a better understanding of God and their purpose in life. I believe that The Revelare contains truths hidden in plain sight that have the potential to change lives for the better and to empower a whole new generation of Christians with the ability to positively affect the world they live in. Bold claims, I know, but I have seen the transformative effect of these truths on ordinary lives.

Revelare is Latin for "reveal." This book reveals some very simple, yet powerful ideas. But those ideas only have the power to change your life when you set aside old assumptions and embrace the truth that has been hiding in plain sight. This book is a journey that I would like to take with you. It's more than just a book of ideas. It is a book of principles that will improve every aspect of your life through the power of a loving God.

Paul K. Lott, Sr.
Author

Paul K. Lott, Sr.

The Revelare
Truths Hidden In Plain Sight

The Revelare

Paul K. Lott, Sr.

Chapter One
Caelum ET Infernum

I believe there is an afterlife. I believe there is a Heaven. In fact, I would say that, in my heart, I know there is a Heaven. I have had too many experiences that leave me no doubt about the afterlife. I also think that most people have no idea of what Heaven is or the purpose of Heaven. Heaven is probably the most important idea at the heart of Christianity and the great motivator that drives most people to religion. After all, Christ came to prepare a place for us in Heaven, right? The very goal of Christianity is to make it to Heaven. The very meaning of what it is to be "saved" is to be selected for admittance into Heaven, yet most people never take the time to understand what the Bible teaches us about Heaven. Most people just accept that, whatever it is, it must be really great.

I heard many different stories about Heaven growing up. As a child, and the son of a minister, I was told that Heaven is a place where Christians go when they die as a reward for their faith. From others, I was told that Heaven was a reward for living a good life. Still others described Heaven as a place where God sends those He loves, and because God loves everyone and forgives everyone,

Heaven is a place where everybody goes! Unless you were really, really bad of course.

Some see Heaven as a highly restricted place reserved for those who follow a certain creed. Many Christians and Muslims hold this view. They often preach a doctrine that is based on fearing Hell rather than a doctrine that is based on loving God. Even those within these religions disagree over which members of their own groups meets the criteria for Heaven. I have attended churches that claimed that members of a church across the street were not real Christians and would not make it to Heaven. I have also been to churches who accept all sects of the Christian faith as candidates for Heaven, regardless of church affiliation. The conflict over the afterlife is equally as contentious among the Muslim population. Beliefs about who will go to Heaven vary broadly from the most restrictive to the most liberal and inclusive points of view.

Most people I know have a problem with Heaven not being for everyone. This belief is held because most people cannot see a loving God condemning anyone to a life of torment in Hell for not accepting a particular creed. They see people more or less living decent lives, trying to survive and care for their families as best they can. They see people putting in a sincere effort to be "good." They see people doing what "feels good" without trying to hurt anyone. I can understand the problem that people have when imagining their families and friends being punished in such a horrible (and eternal) way for failing to embrace a matter of religious doctrine. It is emotionally difficult to understand and embrace a God who would mark people we regard as basically decent as deserving to burn in Hell for all eternity. For most people, it is impossible to accept. It often causes people to reject Christianity and religion altogether as a belief, based on a cruel and unfair God. I would say that conflicting views of Heaven lie at the heart of why most people embrace or reject the Christian or Muslim faiths, and religion in general.

I am proudly a Christian, but I don't share the strict view that Heaven is a reward for accepting a particular creed. That said, I would never say that Heaven is a place for everyone. In fact, I would say that most people who call themselves Christians won't make it to Heaven regardless of their confessed creed. When I say this, most of my religious friends look at me as if I have betrayed the faith. Well, at least until they hear all of what I have to say on the subject. Then they quietly agree. Intellectual belief in the Bible is not enough to earn a place in Heaven. Verbally acknowledging Christ as your savior will not guarantee you a spot in Heaven. Intellectual belief in Christ is not a ticket to Heaven. Heaven is much more than a peaceful place where we go after we die. Heaven is God's home.

Pathway To Heaven

When I teach on Heaven, I always begin with asking my students a question. I ask, "How many of you invite strangers into your home to live, eat your food, and sleep in your bed?" The answer is always the same. None. Then I ask, "How many of you invite friends or strangers to live in your home who won't learn or understand the house rules? Do you invite violent people? Do you welcome liars and the dishonest? Do you welcome thieves? Do you invite people who have no respect for others and the rules of the house?" I get the same answer. None. I then ask them if they would welcome really bad people who always said they were really sorry. Same answer. None. I end with the question, "Well, if you won't do these things, why would God?"

Heaven, basically, is God's home, the place where He lives. It is not a place to reward anyone for anything. It is a place where the people He knows, and who follow His house rules, go to live in peace. It is their common values and character that makes this home into Heaven. Being a nice person or asking God for forgiveness does not earn you a place in Heaven. The only thing that earns anyone a place in Heaven is to possess what I call "Heavenly Character." If most of the people who felt they belonged in Heaven were allowed in, Heaven would be no better than Earth. Heaven is not a place where we improve our character. Heaven is a place where we gather to live with others of like character, godly character. Jesus said it best, "The kingdom of Heaven is within." Heaven must already be a part of you before you can reach its gates. In your heart, you must already possess Heavenly Character before the invitation is given. When Christ taught what we call "The Lord's Prayer," he makes this clear when he teaches us to pray, "Thy kingdom come, Thy will be done on Earth as it is in Heaven." Christ constantly pointed to this idea that Heaven is a state of being here on Earth and his Father's House is just a gathering place for those who have achieved Heaven in their hearts here on Earth.

This is the only view of Heaven that makes sense. Heaven can only be filled with loving people if they were loving before they got there. If God could wave His magic wand and make everyone loving anyway, why would He bother with giving us an earthly life? Godly character is developed through experience and learning, and not through magic. Christ never came to grant us a magical and easy way to skip to the front of the Heaven line. Christ repeatedly stated that what we do as a reflection of personal character will determine the outcome of our lives. Faith is a tool for growth, not the end goal. People learn best from people whom they have faith in. Without trust that God is teaching you what is best, one could never learn what Heavenly Character is. Forgiveness only applies to those mistakes and offenses committed along the path to developing Heavenly Character. Surrendering to habitual moral weakness, and then asking God for forgiveness, results in a denial of that forgiveness. There is no compromise on this principle.

Heaven Is a Voluntary Arrangement

I was always taught that once you made it to Heaven, you were there for all eternity. But, the Bible does not support this idea. We have no example of the dead going to

Heaven and remaining there, but we do have examples of beings who lived in Heaven with God being forced to leave when they no longer agreed with God and no longer wished to honor the house rules. They are called Fallen Angels, or the Fallen, for short.

The Bible tells the story of Lucifer and a group of angels who decided to rebel against God. God, being all knowing, obviously knew that some of His angels were unhappy. He allowed them to discuss their feelings with each other. He allowed them to make their own personal decisions about how they wanted to live their lives. When they decided that they no longer chose to live by the house rules, He did what He never wanted to do. He cast them out of His house to live a life apart from His presence. Lucifer became Satan and, with one third of the angels, God allowed him to leave.

The story is important because it destroys the myth that free will goes away once we make it to Heaven. It turns out that Heaven is a voluntary arrangement. The story illustrates that if we meet the criteria to live with God in His house, we can always change our minds. Going to Heaven does not take away our opinions or ability to think independently. Being in Heaven does not make us God's programmed army. Heaven is God's home, and those who are invited choose to be there and choose to live in such a way as to preserve its peace and harmony.

Seeing Is Not Believing

Most people who hear the story of the fall of Satan and the Fallen never stop to ask important questions about God, Heaven, and eternal life. These questions are important because they define our purpose for life in THIS realm of existence. A person blindly following a set of religious doctrines or creeds would no more be worthy to live in God's home any more than a convicted serial killer. Heaven is bigger than all that. Heaven is not a reward. Heaven is an invitation to live in the presence of God in a family relationship based on trust and free will.

Lucifer lived with God, as did the other Fallen. They were constantly in His presence, yet even in His presence, they came to disagreement with God. It was not an isolated incident, but a group incident. We don't have an exact count, but a fair number of the angels, from discussions among themselves, decided that they did not want what God had to offer. They wanted to embrace another way. That way led them to being cast out. Even more, God, being a God of love, must have been deeply affected by the loss of so many He loved. It is that loss that led to our way of life, to be raised apart from God's presence only to learn the desire to remain in His presence for all eternity. At the end of the day, the central lesson of Satan's choice is that seeing is not believing. The Fallen saw God anytime they desired, yet they lost their belief in Him. Our journey, in this realm, is to learn to believe, so that we can learn to clearly see.

We are born weak and defenseless, relying entirely on the love of our parents to sustain us until we are able to learn to struggle through life on our own. We are separated from the Face of God and are condemned to experience God through faith alone. In reality, everything we do is dependent on our "faith eyes" because we have the ability to prove very little beyond a doubt. When a parent goes off to work, children take it on faith that the parent will return. Without this faith, we would have been wrecked as individuals. Once we are past our childhood years of extreme dependence, we are faced with moral questions of conduct that often seem to have no clear answers. Many of us do our best to learn by trial and error, while others learn to rely on the advice and wisdom of elders. Eventually, we come to some kind of a moral standard by which we live. It is this standard of life that eventually becomes the measure by which we are found suitable or unsuitable to live in God's presence.

Seeing is not believing. Believing is seeing. When we believe in a way of life, it guides our steps, and the steps we take define the person we become. The Fallen lived in God's presence, but they did not see Him. The heart of "The Revelare," the revealing, is that we must first learn to SEE God before we are allowed to be WITH God. The reason I wrote this book is to give you some insights on how to successfully make that journey to God. Without this "Heavenly Character" no one makes it to Heaven regardless of religious creed, or lack thereof.

The Problem with Hell

Most of what we think about Hell comes from a fictional novel written during the Middle Ages called Dante's Inferno. The images and ideas from the medieval work has captured the imagination of countless authors and movie producers, but its contents bear little basis in the Bible. In the Gospels, Jesus never actually talked about Hell as most of us understand it. In fact, he did not use the word "Hell" at all, though it is often translated as such. Instead, he used a word that means "garbage dump." The garbage dump was a place outside the city walls where the refuse was disposed of.

Undesirable people and criminals were also forced to live outside the city walls. What Jesus actually talked about is Gehenna, and his core teaching is that those who reject God are merely condemned to live separately from God. "Hell", according to Christ, is having to live outside of God's presence.

Christ's definition of "Hell" is just. Most would agree that those who choose not to accept God, and choose another path, should be free to live apart from Him. This is a natural consequence of that choice. Jesus teaches that those who chose to live lawlessly cannot live among the lawful. Their "punishment" is not enacted at the hands of a vengeful God. Their punishment is to live among others who also reject God. We find in the Bible Book of Revelation that only the worst and most violent Fallen were locked away in fiery pits. The rest were free to roam outside of Heaven, outside of the city walls. It is important to understand that the punishment of being separated is reasonable. It is the same standard that our society goes by today. Those who reject the laws of a society are also forced to live outside of that society.

Free Will at the Heart of Love

God gives every person free will. There is no mandate that any of us reside in Heaven when the time comes. Free will is at the heart of love. God could have programmed everyone to only do what He deemed as good. He could have created people that were always obedient and always agreed with Him. But, He did not create us as virtual robots because, without choice, there cannot be true love. The reason why the love of a friend, your spouse, or that of your children is so meaningful is because love is largely voluntary. Love is something we choose to give or withhold. We feel happy when someone chooses to love us. It is the same with God. He loved us by choice and the only love He wants in return is the love we choose to give. That means there is always the risk that we won't love Him. Whether we reside in Heaven or live separated from God, love demands the same from everyone. Love demands that it be given by our choosing. That is why the Fallen were allowed to choose. It is why we are here on this Earth, burdened with a life made of the choices we make in all of our relationships.

Choice is a double-edged sword, however, because it means everyone around us also has the same power to choose. Others may choose to love us less or not at all. But, when mutual love is chosen, that love changes the dynamic of how we treat one another. Love changes the "house rules" we follow in the relationship. With a chosen love comes the demand for honesty, loyalty, and belief in and from the one we choose to love. When we love, our expectations change completely. We demand more because love makes our hearts need more. Love makes us vulnerable to pain and suffering when the other person does not return genuine love. But, when we learn to love more fully because of our choice to love, it changes the way we act and makes us see things in others that we would not have noticed otherwise.

God's Universal Will

In Matthew 7:21–23, Jesus declares to amazed listeners, "Not everyone who says to me, 'Lord, Lord,' will enter the kingdom of Heaven, but only the one who does the will of my Father who is in Heaven. Many will say to me on that day, 'Lord, Lord, did we not prophesy in your name and in your name drive out demons and in your name perform many miracles?' Then I will tell them plainly, 'I never knew you. Away from me, you evildoers!'"

Honestly, this passage confused me for years. Here, Jesus is talking about someone who did miracles and cast out demons. To me, that sounded like a pretty good person, considering I had never done any of these things. Frankly, when I read this passage, it scared me. Could I ever be good enough? It wasn't until I was older and recognized that the key to Heaven was in actions that proceeded from the will of God, and not just on good actions themselves. People do good things for all kinds of reasons, but not every reason is rooted in true godliness. To do any good in the absence of love is clearly the same as doing evil in God's eyes. God is love, and His actions toward each of us are a reflection of His love. His will for each of us is a reflection of His love. The only acceptable actions we can take on His behalf are those actions that proceed from true love. Everything you do must proceed from love to be acceptable to God. I know of many churches that push their members to focus on obedience rather than understanding and love. In the short term, these efforts produce results. People become more obedient to the Word of God. The problem is that none of these blind acts of obedience results in a heart for God, compliance with His will, or a pathway to Heaven. You would want to live with people who love you, not people who pretend to love you because they are afraid of the circumstances. Why expect God to live by a lower standard?

Finally, to those who hold that a rigid belief in Christ qualifies you for Heaven. Paul writes in his letter to the Romans 2:13–16:

"For it is not those who hear the law who are righteous in God's sight, but it is those who obey the law who will be declared righteous. (Indeed, when Gentiles, who do not have the law, do by nature things required by the law, they are a law for themselves, even though they do not have the law. They show that the requirements of the law are written on their hearts, their consciences also bearing witness, and their thoughts sometimes accusing them and at other times even defending them.) This will take place on the day when God judges people's secrets through Jesus Christ, as my gospel declares."

Paul makes the obvious statement that those who DO what God asks are declared righteous. But then he adds the curious statement about Gentiles, or those outside the religious fold. He states that those who do not know the law (Bible/God's commands), but act in a way that reflects what God wants them to do anyway, are acceptable to God because in the absence of the written word (Bible), they do the things written in the Bible. Paul teaches that God has placed a sense of right and wrong in everyone's heart, and that those who listen to God in the form of their conscience are in a relationship with God. They are therefore acceptable because of their obedience to God. Ignorance of the law, or the written word in the Bible, leaves no one an excuse! If we have not destroyed our conscience through wrongdoing, and if we listen to God speaking to us through conscience, we can develop Heavenly Character by living according to what God has placed in our hearts. This is not to say that we should do what "feels good." This passage is saying that we all know inside what God wants and can respond even when we are ignorant of what is written. If we understand this, we understand that God is, in fact,

15

loving and just. He gives everyone an opportunity for Heaven. Though those with knowledge of God hold the advantage, the religious and the non-religious stand on the same ground and must live by the same standard.

Mea Soleat

I grew up in a large family. My parents had eight kids. Growing up in my large family, everybody had somebody. I had my dad. I protected my younger brother, but my dad was my closest friend. Siblings are not always the nicest to each other, and I was more than a bit odd, so I was not well liked. I wasn't close to any of my siblings except my younger brother. I read books instead of playing with toys. I was tall for my age, so many kids in my neighborhood were too intimated to want to play sports with me. I always won. Instead, I followed my dad around as much as I could on Saturdays and Sundays after church. He was a minister. He trusted me to teach the second grade Sunday school class even though I was only in the fifth grade myself, and he showed a lot of pride in my academic focus. I went with him when he went to houses to counsel couples. I would watch the kids. While my brothers and sisters were busy being kids and teens, I was with my dad . . . or reading. That all changed when I was eleven years old, just before my twelfth birthday.

I remember walking home from school with one of my friends, and when I turned the corner I saw an ambulance in front of our home about two blocks away. I didn't think much of it. I thought that a church member had fallen ill while visiting my dad. I arrived home to find that it was my dad who had fallen ill. Within a few weeks, my mom told our family that my dad had cancer and would not live much longer.

Over the next six months, I spent a lot of time traveling with my mom to cancer centers. We got snowed in a few times, and I found myself sleeping in my dad's room to keep him company. I skipped school a lot the rest of the year to stay with my dad. He told me stories. He talked of the challenges he had lived through in his life, and the ones I should avoid. I understood later that he was giving me a long goodbye. Before that time, I was emotionally tough at times and utterly clueless at others. I did not cry much until then. But, during those six months leading up to his death, I cried a lot. I was not one to cry in front of people. I knew I could never let my younger brother see me cry or it would upset him too much. So I would go for a run every day and found it was the best time to cry.

Those six months put me face-to-face with death and the afterlife. My dad's time was coming to an end, and I could not avoid the questions raised about my faith. That was the year I started to study the Bible. I needed some comfort. My heart was breaking and I did not know how I would survive my dad's passing because I felt that once he was gone, I would have no one.

My dad died in June of that year. He waited for my aunt to arrive to comfort my mother and then he let go. The day he died, we were preparing to go to the hospital to see him.

The broken alarm on the kitchen stove went off loudly. Not only was it broken, it was unplugged. I knew in my heart that my dad was gone. I felt panicked.

We all arrived at the hospital to the news that he had, in fact, died at the same time the stove alarm started ringing. I remember being led into the waiting room that was next to his room at the Veterans' Hospital in Wilkes-Barre, PA. Everyone started crying, but I found I could not. I had to see him so I slipped into his room to see his face. I remember the way the room smelled. I remember what his face looked like. I remember seeing a shadow waving over his face. I knew it was my dad, waving goodbye to me. It was then that I could cry alone, holding my dad's hand. I felt like I was suffocating because I could not catch my breath. I remember hearing someone come into the room and feeling the need to not show any tears. My heart broke even more as I watched my sisters and little brother cry. My mother had silent tears. She held her head down, as I held to her side. While helping her care for my dad as he died, she had become the friend to replace the one I had just lost.

My dad made my mom a promise. He told her that if God would not forbid it, he would let her know if he was okay. Over the next month, we would see my dad many times, or see small things that allowed him to keep his word. The last memory I have of my dad was of him sitting on the bed as he always did after work. He looked at me and then he was gone. I never saw him again, but I knew that he had reached us from the afterlife. That is why I know that our life does not end with our time here. My dad showed me that. From his wave goodbye to the final time I saw his face, he wanted all of us to know that things don't end with death.

The Revelare

Chapter Two
Librum

The Bible is the most widely distributed book in the world and a perennial best seller. Sadly, the Bible is also the least read book in the world in proportion to the number of books sold. And I believe the Bible is the most misunderstood book in the world.

A story I love to tell is about a wife making a ham on Christmas Eve. Her husband watches as she trims the ends of the ham before putting it in the oven. The husband asks, "Why do you trim off the ends of the ham?" His wife says, "I don't know. My mom always did." Because she was curious as well, she calls her mother to ask. But her mother doesn't know either. Her mother says, "My mother always did it, so that is how I do it. That is why I taught you." Wanting to know the answer, she gets her grandmother on the phone on a three-way call with her mother to find out why she trimmed the ends of her hams. On hearing the question, the grandmother bursts into laughter before answering, "I would cut the ends of the ham because it was too big to fit into my tiny oven." For most people, the Bible is the same. Ideas have been passed down for so long, their original meanings have been lost, and no one remembers why certain things were done. They just repeat them.

The Bible as a Sacred Document

Today, the Bible is a sacred document, and is endowed with almost magical powers. People who have never, nor will ever, read the Bible would swear that the Bible is the absolute, unquestioned truth. What the Bible is has long been forgotten and has been replaced with the image of a book of magic, rather than just a collection of meaningful letters and writings authored by flesh and blood believers. So much effort is spent 'respecting' the Bible, few bother to actually read the Bible. Most people simply accept what they are told by their religious leaders and never suspect that their leaders are likely repeating the doctrine of their church organization without respect for actual Bible content.

At its heart, the Bible is a witness document. That is the true basis for its authority. Something happened. Someone wrote it down to let others know about it. These writings were passed from person to person, and church to church over centuries. The Bible is not even a book; rather, it is a collection of books and letters composed by independent writers recording or responding to the events of their time. This process took several thousand years to complete. The only unifying thread of these documents is that the writers are adding their personal stories of how their faith in God was being played out on life's stage. Most people don't realize that agreement on what documents would be included in the Bible was not decided until well after the third century AD. For over three hundred years after the death and resurrection of Christ, there was no agreement among believers as to what books and letters were sacred. In fact, worldwide, there is still not absolute agreement on what documents constitute the Bible today. There are many churches that have more than the sixty-six documents commonly accepted.

Christians claim the Bible as the basis of their beliefs. It is respected as the source of truth for the church and the document of its guiding principles. Yet the divisions among the Christian community over Bible teachings are troubling. When I was in the fifth grade, I remember asking my dad, "If all churches go by the Bible, why are there so many different churches teaching so many different things? Why don't they just sit down and read it together to unite all Christians?" My dad wasn't prepared for this question, and after fumbling for words, finally settled with telling me that it was not possible, and I would understand when I got older.

My dad was right. I would understand it when I got older. I have had many friends who were pastors, and I have met a lot of Bible scholars over the years. What I learned was that all of them had spent a lot of time reading books about the Bible, and almost no time reading the Bible. I have not met a single pastor who has been able to tell me that they read the entire Bible even once from beginning to end. As with any book, if I sit down and read pieces of the book out of order, I can never get the full message of the book, and without that full message, I could never understand how any of these very dedicated men found it possible to put their trust in books someone else had written about the Bible.

There is a statement often used in many churches, "The Bible is the inerrant Word of God." The statement conjures up images of holy men, with pen in hand, writing the words of the Bible with the Holy Spirit looking over their shoulders to guide what words are to be written on the sacred pages. At the end of that process, we have a book "inspired" by the Holy Spirit and sacred for all Christians. The problem is that this scenario never took place.

Origin of the Bible

To understand the Bible and understand its teachings, I think it is important that we first understand where the Bible came from. The Bible is composed of sixty-six books including the thirty-nine books of the Jewish Bible and twenty-seven books of the New Testament. These sixty-six books comprise the collection of documents modern Christians regard as authoritative for faith and inspired by God. These sixty-six documents were not compiled into a complete list until sometime around 367 AD.

How the list was selected in not entirely clear. There were many more documents circulating in the early churches that never made the list. Some were excluded because they were incomplete. For example, there were other gospel accounts known to the early church, but many were fragments and repeated information already contained in the gospels we know of today, so they were not included. Other documents were obviously written much later and contained some church doctrine combined with mythical or fictional stories. Other documents were not included because they contained doctrinal problems, or were not deemed to contain useful information.

Generally, the primary criterion when evaluating a document for inclusion in the Bible was that it be an accurate witness from the earliest knowable date. If a document was known to be circulated over many generations and was found to be useful or accepted as authentic by a broad population of the church, then the document would be considered authentic and a candidate for the Bible. Despite what many ministers will admit, the Bible does contain many contradictions that cannot be explained away as mysteries of the Holy Spirit. These contradictions don't, however, decrease the importance of what the Bible contains. These contradictions are the reason why the Bible has more credibility.

Bible as a Witness Document

We know that witnesses of the same event never report exactly the same account of an incident. In the Bible, we have four gospel accounts by four different writers written over an unknown span of time covering the first century AD. Each of them contains a slightly different account of events, as a witness record should. In reality, witnesses to the same event rarely recall or report the event in identical terms. When recording witness reports, there can be considerable differences in the recall that each witness reports. Those collecting witnesses' accounts understand that they will produce slightly different versions of what happened. It is the same with the Bible. There should be contradictions and inconsistencies in the text because real witnesses don't report identical versions of an event. The collectors of the Bible understood this simple truth. That all of the documents agreeing was not something that burdened their decision-making process. Their focus was on whether the community at large had accepted these documents over a long period of time and found them useful. To them, broad consensus was the only evidence of "divine inspiration."

As far as we know, most of the original apostles could not write well enough to record anything. Matthew, because of his career as a tax collector, may have been literate enough, but the rest are questionable. That is the reason we don't have a large body of documents written by the apostles themselves. Fortunately, the number of disciples was much larger than the twelve disciples/apostles of Jesus's inner circle. Stories of events would have been written down and collected over time by groups of followers looking to preserve accurate accounts of what happened. The writer of Luke and Acts does not even claim to be a witness to the things he wrote in the gospel he authored. In fact, the Gospel of Luke is not a book at all. It is a letter written to a Roman leader to convert him to Christianity. Luke was a physician and a gentile (non-Jew) who was not present to witness the events he wrote about. Acts was a continuation of Luke's letter. All the writings of Paul are letters to churches he had visited, with the exception of the letter he wrote to the church at Rome. Paul was not trying to write scripture, or contribute to the Bible. He was writing letters to people he knew, addressing situations that he needed to address among the church congregations he had planted. A number of books, including Revelation remained in serious doubt by the early church, and still remains in question by modern day scholars. Over time, all of these facts were forgotten, and the sixty-six documents of the Bible took on an almost magical quality. People stopped reading the letters and books as intended, and started to extract passages they deemed most useful or that supported their particular view of Christian doctrine. When the writers of the Bible talk about scriptures, they are talking about what we would consider the Old Testament. At the time they wrote, they were largely unaware of most of the other documents we deem as sacred.

The Problem with Peter and the Reason for the Bible

I need to address an argument to the point I made above. In II Peter 3:16, "Peter" writes of Paul, "He writes the same way in all his letters, speaking in them of these matters. His letters contain some things that are hard to understand, which ignorant and unstable people distort, as they do the other Scriptures, to their own destruction." I have often heard this as an argument that Peter was identifying the writings of Paul as scripture. This is not the case. II Peter was one of the last letters included in the New Testament because of doubts about its authenticity noted by early church leaders. They deemed the doubts not enough to bar its inclusion in the Bible. II Peter heavily relies on Jude and the Book of Enoch for its content. Enoch was excluded from the Bible. I Peter and II Peter were not even written by the same writer. In order for II Peter to be authentic, it would have had to be written before Peter's death between 65–67 AD. In order to make informed references to the letters of Paul, it had to have been completed before 60 AD for Peter to even have common knowledge of Paul's letters. Fed Ex didn't exist back then. Things took time. It is most likely that II Peter was written between 100–150 AD. That is far too late for a true Peter authorship. Additionally, one of the core issues addressed in II Peter was not an issue during Peter's life, namely the seeming delay of the second coming of Christ. Concern regarding the delay in the return of Christ was not a concern until the early second century. II Peter may be a witness document, but it is not Peter's witness. Almost two thousand years later, the average Christian reads this passage as affirmation that Peter recognized the writings of Paul as Holy Scripture, but when II Peter was accepted as part of the Bible, it served the purpose of reinforcing the fourth-century need to put a blanket of sacredness over the entire collections of selected documents to halt the recognition of more questionable (and later) documents as sacred.

By the end of the first century, all the direct witnesses to the life of Christ had died, leaving behind a church struggling to maintain itself under new leadership and broad persecution. Jerusalem was destroyed, and the apostles who had walked with Jesus were dead without leaving much of a written record. The documents of the Bible were collected out of necessity. In the early days of the church, it was almost commonplace for writers to create documents claiming apostolic authorship. The church leaders became concerned with ideas they considered heretical and wanted to seal the number of writings to be considered as authoritative for church teachings. Efforts had started around 200 AD to compile a list of trusted documents, but the collection we know as the Bible today would not be finalized for more than a century and a half later.

The Problem with the Romans

Deviation from the original focus of Jesus's ministry began toward the end of the first century. The early church was largely maintained via an oral tradition, meaning teachings were by word of mouth. Very little was written down. Once the Jerusalem church was destroyed in 70 AD, the Jewish church was scattered. With it, the direct oral teachings of Jesus were scattered. Within a generation, the shift of Christian beliefs would move from its Jewish centric thought to the pagan centric thought of the Roman Empire.

The Roman religious thinking was very different from the Jewish religious thinking. Roman religious thought was based on a contractual relationship with their many gods. Romans were not spiritual at all and only looked to religion as a practical matter. Their religious practices largely resolved around rituals that served the purpose of appeasing their gods or currying favor with them. Their gods were not concerned with individual moral conduct, but rather, acted like self-absorbed men. Roman religious life consisted of a number of domestic rituals and prayers absent a moral code. Over time, mainstream Christianity would move in the same direction. Modern Christianity is centered on rituals and the prayer reading. Compared to what is written in the Bible, our Christian religious practices would be almost unrecognized as Christian by Christ himself. Christ would see a largely Roman religion with a loose (very loose) relationship to his teachings. When I say "largely Roman" I am not just talking about the Roman Catholic Church. I am talking about nearly all-mainstream churches today including evangelical churches. Like a Roman religion, modern Christianity focuses on "the grand bargain." Accept Christ (without really defining what that means), get baptized, and you will be "saved." Once "saved," church attendance, tithing, communion, and a number of other rituals bind you. Prayers are prewritten and repeated in groups. If you mess up, just say you are sorry and all is forgiven. We gather for a meeting. We leave the meeting. And like the Romans, Christianity becomes "practical" and we all get to go to "Heaven." The rituals allow us to curry favor with God. The rituals make us feel better about ourselves. When we are in trouble, we can call on God for help. I used to say that most Christians see God as a cosmic Santa Claus. Today, Christian living is comprised mostly of paying our respects to God, rather than working to become better people. Christian groups spend more time arguing over who is right on a particular document, rather than caring for each other, and the poor, as Christ commanded.

Fortunately for all of us, the teachings of Christ are preserved in the Bible, even if they are more of a background noise at times. When the teachings of the New Testament are contrasted to the teachings of the Old Testament, the message is lost. God did not change who He was for a non-Jewish audience. Much of the New Testament is filtered through a Roman lens shaping the image of God presented in the writings. Paul is the author of most of the New Testament writings, and as such sets the larger perspective of how God is presented. Paul was Jewish, but he was also a Roman citizen (which was never explained). Paul needed to present the gospel in a way that appealed to a non-Jewish audience. He presented Jewish ideas in a Roman context. Jesus taught for three years, but Paul was not a follower of Christ while He lived. Paul did not have the benefit of living in Jesus's inner circle. Paul presents the gospel through a Roman lens, and only heard the teachings of Christ secondhand. Paul was literate and a competent organizer. And so, the church communities that were largely preserved were communities founded by Paul. Organizers tend to win when it comes to history.

That said, Paul's writings are still the witness documents of a man committed to spreading the gospel of Christ, and as such they preserve very important teachings. Reading all of the writings of the Bible informs our faith because it takes us into the lives of those who have experienced many of the same struggles that we have experienced. But it is a wrong use of the Bible to focus on scripture and verse (largely out of historical and situational context), which restricts God. When reading the Bible, stop trying to be so preoccupied with its sacred status and pay more attention to what the writers were trying to communicate about their spiritual journey. Let the voices of the past speak to you. The Bible can be messy at times, and hard to understand, but it is our guide to discovering a closer walk with God.

Chapter Three

Initium

There is a difference between doubting and asking questions. Doubt is an issue of belief. Questioning is an issue of understanding. When I was young, I did not doubt the reality of God. I tried. I remember thinking to myself that I would just stop believing in God and see what would happen... what it would feel like. The experiment ended very quickly because my next thought was that I could not pretend there is no God. In my heart, I knew that God was real. That belief, however, did not put to rest the questions I wanted to ask.

I asked a lot of the standard questions that most people think of at some point or another... Why does God let bad things happened, etc? But the one that really stuck in my head for some time was, 'why us'? Why bother? What I had taken from all the church and Bible reading I had done up until then was that God spent a lot of time preoccupied with the moral condition of man, and I wanted to know why? To say He loves us brings the same question...why? I reasoned at the time that to understand why, I had to go back to the beginning.

When you are told what a document says over and over, there comes a point at which you stop listening to what you are reading and begin to substitute the ideas you are taught in place of what you are reading. I had read the story of the creation of man many times, but this time, I realized that I was only repeating in my mind, the things I had already been taught. I wanted to empty my head completely of what I thought I knew to see what I could learn. So I took on the task of rereading the Bible with an empty mind.

The first thing that I noticed was that the creation of man was very different then all of the other acts of creation in the Bible. It does not matter whether you accept the creation story literally or not. What matters is that you understand what the writer is trying to say about our place with God and in the world.

God created everything by command until it came to the creation of Man. Like poetry, the story echoes God commanding things into existence as He shaped the world into a place suitable for Man. The pages echo, "And God said, 'Let there be… Let there be… Let there be…'." But when it came to Man, God paused. He took the time to form a human body with His own hands. I thought to myself that this was a very intimate act of creation as He formed the curves of the man's face and body with His own fingers. Once He had created a body, His act of creation did not conclude with God commanding life into Man. Instead, it ended with an even more intimate act. The Bible records that God breathed into Man the 'Breathe of Life' and that Man become a living soul.

Growing up, I took the term 'Breathe of Life' in the same way I viewed one person breathing air into another person's lungs. I thought a 'magical breathe of air' gave life to Man. On this reading, what struck me is that this view made no sense. God does not literally breathe. God is Spirit. The Hebrew word translated as 'Breathe of Life' is ruach. Ruach is used in many forms in the Bible, but all of it's uses share a common thread. Ruach is an term referring to an aspect or naming of God's Spirit. Ruach Elohim means 'Spirit of God'. 'The Spirit of the Lord' is written as 'Ruach Adonai'. 'Holy Spirit' is 'Ruach Hakkodesh'. Finally, Ruach-El means the Spirit of God. The Book of Job uses this form in Job 33:4, 'The Spirit of God hath made me, and the breath of the Almighty has given me life.

A Personal Act of God

What I realized that day was that something very personal had happened in the creation of Man. I was not sure if the term 'creation' could express the idea of what actually happened in the Bible. If we understand that Ruach is God's Spirit than we see a very different story. We see God preparing a physical body to contain a soul that would come directly from God's very own Soul. We see an act of active birth and not an act of passive creation. We see God creating a child in much the same way that our parents 'created' us; two parts combining for new life, Earth and Spirit. We see God breaking off a part of Himself to create His living child.

Whenever I have taught this truth, those who have strong church ties challenge the idea. In church, we are always taught of how worthless we are and how we need God to make us better. Many religious people find it very difficult to accept that the bond between Man and God is more intimate that they were taught. But, if we are honest with ourselves, nothing less makes sense. It makes sense and the clues to this truth are riddled throughout the Bible. Many of these clues were highlighted by Jesus himself.

As the story goes, it was during the winter Festival of Dedication in Jerusalem. The Jewish leaders of the day had approached Jesus to stone him. Jesus asked them what good thing had he done as the reason for being stoned. The leaders answered that it was not for the good works he was doing that they wanted to stone him, but because he claimed to be God. Jesus corrected them on two accounts. First he pointed out that the scriptures called them 'gods'. (Psalm 82:6) Second, he reminded them that he had not said he was God. Jesus had said he was the 'Son of God'. So Jesus's logic was to ask the leaders why they were upset with him saying that he was the Son of God when the Bible already made it clear that they were all god's (little g). The Jewish leaders considered it blasphemy to claim such an intimate link to God. Jesus made it clear that his claim was no big deal because they as gods too shared in that intimate relationship with God.

Another proof that comes to mind is the story of the Prodigal Son. Jesus never told the story of the Prodigal Adopted Son. Jesus tells the story of a son who leaves home, losses his way in the world, and then finally realizes his sins and returns to his father's house. What is clear is that this is the story of a blood family member returning home. There is a wealth of evidence in the Bible to support this view, but the greatest proof is in looking inside ourselves.

The Apples Close to the Tree

Everything that God wants, we want. Everything that God craves, we crave. God is love, and He seeks a loving relationship with us. It is almost an obsession. Over thousands of years, the Bible plays out this story of God's constant reaching out to Mankind despite our regular rejection of Him and His teachings. He, the Creator, seems to beg and plead at times for man to embrace Him. He sends prophets to encourage us back to Him. He even sent a Messiah to bridge the gap between Himself and Mankind. He did this, and continues to this day, because of His intense love for His children and the desire to see them grow to their full potential.

My detractors will point out the Bible also says that belief in Christ or obedience to God gives people the 'right to be called the Children of God." This does not mean that we are not already His actual children. In human relationships, if a family member is doing something shameful against the family's sense of decency, parents, siblings, and other relatives often declare that the offending family member is no longer counted as part of that family. Because of their conduct, a family member can loose the right to be called a member of the family. In the same way, when a person behaves in a way approved of by God, He gives them the right to take up their rightful name as His child. He gives them the right to be called the children of God. Jesus is first born among many brothers and sisters (Romans 8:29).

The Nature of Love

When you love someone deeply, you want that someone to love you back. God asks you to love Him with all of your heart, soul, and strength because He loves you with ALL of His heart, soul, and strength. His desire to be involved in your life is a natural consequence of His love for His children. When we really understand this truth and take it to heart, we understand God so much more, and we understand our own desire and craving for love. We start to understand that He is the source, and that the only way we can ever find our place, our purpose, and eternal contentment is to embrace His nature as the source of our nature.

I had discovered the answer to why, but like so many things in life, one answered question gives rise to many more questions. For me, I had to fundamentally reprogram my thinking about my potential as God saw me. I remember thinking that when people fail, they say, 'I am only human'. In the light of who we are, to associate failure with human nature is wrong. Instead, when we fall short of God's expectations, we are failing to be human as He intended humanity to be.

The essence of God's nature is love. That being said, it makes sense that we have a special need for love in our lives. The start of all human suffering and unhappiness is a lack of love. Sometimes the issue is that love is not given. At other times, the problem is that love is not understood. Without love, things go wrong inside of us. I believe that this is the root of all problems in the world. But the love I am talking about is not the fairy tale feelings that most people call love. The love that everyone craves is a divine love. This love is accepting, yet calls us higher. Divine love cares for us without needing anything in return. Divine love is a love of self, extended on equal footing to those we claim to love.

We are born with a love of self, driven by our extreme needs. In fact, to our view, the world existed to meet our needs. This is how we first developed our early sense of love. In these early years, we learn to love ourselves, and then we learn to love those who seem to love us as we love ourselves. In the arms of our mothers, we first learn to trust. We learn what it means to be accepted, over time, by the way that she comforts our tears and cares for our needs. Gradually, that circle of love expands, as we grow a little older until finally, person by person, we learned to extend our self love to love of family and finally to love of friends and beyond. This is the normal way of things.

The way I like to explain it is that love starts as a tiny circle. At first, this circle only has room enough for one person; oneself. Gradually that circle starts to expand to family, then to friends, then to more and more people. As the circle expands, our sense of love grows and we have balance. The circle does not grow unconditionally. The circle expands in a delicate dance between love given, love wanted, and then love received. With each cycle, the balance of our life expands. We give love and want to be loved in return. When our love is accepted and returned, the cycle is complete and then a new cycles begins. Along the road of life, interruption of this cycle is inevitable. When this cycle breaks down or becomes corrupted, we start to twist inside and we start to look for substitutions for the real love. We embrace the things that make us feel loved, even when we know that love is false. When the love cycle breaks down, we start to retreat toward a circle of one. The more times we have to retreat, the harder it becomes for us to give and accept true love.

God's love gives us the ability to stand strong when other loves in our lives break down. He is the Source. Our relationship to Him is the reason we need love so much. A relationship with God is as fundamental to our health as that fundamental relationship we had with our mothers immediately after we were born. But, the love of our mothers can only take us so far. At some point, we need bigger arms to carry us the rest of the way.

God as Father

When we have a nurturing relationship with God, the power of His love and acceptance can carry us through the advances and retreats of love in other parts of our lives. When people disappoint us, betray us, and fail to love us, God's love has healing power. It heals our love circle and protects it from shrinking. It gives us the courage to trust enough to seek and accept new love so that throughout our lives, the love in our hearts is constantly growing.

Without God's love, the circle can be broken, and with it, our hearts and our lives. I have seen first hand how twisted people can become when they grow up not feeling that essential love and acceptance. It creates emotional and spiritual cravings that take over that person's life. It is much like a person missing some nutritional need in their bodies. People who have acute nutritional needs have all kinds of odd cravings, and some of those cravings can even grow into full-blown addictions. Often these cravings are not obvious signs of what may be missing. I have known people that crave dirt, baby powder, and a range of other non-food cravings medically related to a missing food nutrient. The spirit works in a similar way. A love deficit can cause a person to crave too much attention in a desperate effort to fill the void. A love deficit can make a person crave sexual experiences because it temporarily feels like love to them. Others do things to starve their need for love by avoiding people and situations that remind them of what they are missing. Love deficits lead to increased stress, medical conditions, mental illness, and are the root of war, poverty, and human suffering. People who have a love deficit can twist their inner emptiness into a need to increase the suffering of others. Those who have a love deficit embrace selfishness as a way of life, and that selfishness goes on to steal the love potential of others.

God is love. We are His children. We are designed to love because that is the nature of our Father. Love is the nature of what was passed down to us in that ruach, that Breathe of Life. Just as the Bible records the story of God chasing His children across time and distance, our lives are a chronicle of our quest for love; to be loved, to give love, to complete the love cycle. Our lives are made up of the people we have loved and who loved us back, as well as those who have rejected us and caused us pain. Our lives are victorious when rejection cannot destroy us because we have a loving foundation in our Father that gives us the confidence to express love freely because we KNOW we are loved by Him.

In beginning, our Father created us. He created us from His own Spirit. The nature of that Spirit passed down to us is a Spirit of love. At the heart of each of us, love is what makes us whole. Stop selling yourself short by being less than what you are. Stop accepting substitutes for love, when your Father gave you the capacity for so much more.

Chapter Four

Pater Meus

For as long as I can remember, I have called God, Father in private. Publicly, I address Father as God because so many people seem confused by my use of Father. I think it was my dad that told me of the Bible verse telling us to called no one Father, but God. In the Bible (Matthew 23:9), Jesus said 'And do not call anyone on Earth 'father,' for you have one Father, and he is in Heaven.' I don't recall when I first heard this, but I know I was very young. It was before I started school. My Dad was pretty firm on this point and I took it to heart.

How we address our Father can color our relationship with Him. God is what He is. Our Father is who He is, and Father is the way He wants to be addressed by His children. Even in the Lord's Prayer, we are taught to say "Our Father, who is in Heaven". Somehow most people miss this fine point. I am sure that it would be odd to call our earthly dad 'Human'. We call him dad because that is who he is to us. In the same way, God is our Father. He wants to be called Father and should be called Father.

Focusing on Father as your parent, rather than a deity, can change your relationship for the better. First of all, your Father wants to be a part of your daily life. 'God' brings with it such formality. Father is far less formal and using the term to address Him can effect your communication with Him in a big way. Father implies a more intimate emotional parent/child relationship. Father implies a far more nurturing relationship then 'God', even if the 'God' relationship is perceived as a loving one. So what makes a good father and how does that measure against our Heavenly Father? What qualities do we look for in a good father?

Good Parenting

Good parenting starts with unconditional acceptance. I have always said that two things are needed to make a relationship truly work: unconditional acceptance and unconditional love. Unconditional acceptance comes first, because until we feel accepted for who we are at that very moment, we have a hard time allowing ourselves to feel love from a person. When we feel accepted, we are open to other things because we are free to express the true side of ourselves, and that side can include an awful lot of flaws. The more insecure we are about ourselves, more important acceptance becomes in our path forward.

In the human parent/child relationship, acceptance is one of the main obstacles to a strong parent/child relationship. As our children start to change as they approach puberty, there is a fear in the heart of our children that the changes and differences in who they are becoming may cause their parents to reject them. I suspect that a barrier to accepting God as Father is the same type of fear. Father accepts everyone for who they are. This does not mean, like a human parent, that He accepts everything His child does. After all, a parent's role is to help a child grow in the right direction. But, what it does mean is that there is nothing that your Father despises so much that He lets it interfere with His recognition and acceptance of you as His child. As a Father who loves, He accepts.

Being a good father is based on love, unconditional love. It is the reason why He accepts you. Some people find it hard to think of themselves as children, but compared to our Father, that is what we are. Because we are His children, He understands that we will make mistakes as we develop the moral character that will bring us to spiritual adulthood. While we may disappoint Him, he keeps loving us and trying to help us grow and learn. He is absolutely committed to helping you to become the best version of yourself you can be. Father does not look down from Heaven in judgment. Instead, He walks beside us as we walk through life, even carrying us at times.

Because our Father loves us unconditionally, He also disciplines us. One of the points I always make when talking about parenting is that there is a difference between discipline and punishment. A parent should only punish a child for acts of willful disobedience. Punishment is just that - punishment. It is the act of depriving a child of something as a punishment for a willful act. Discipline is the act of using a focused action to teach a child a corrective habit.

For example, if my child sneaks out a window to attend a party, it is an act of willful disobedience. In this case, I use punishment. I may ground my child for disobeying my instructions. This is the denying of a privilege as a reminder of your parental authority. If my child lies, I use punishment. I usually deny my child something that directly involves the lie. But, if my child spills a glass of milk or does poorly on a test in school, I use discipline to teach. For spilled milk, I teach the child to place the milk above the plate and I reinforce this habit to avoid placing the milk where it is easily spilled. For a bad test grade, I may increase my child's study time or add additional lessons and reading to support the child's education related habits.

A parent disciplines a child to teach the child the discipline to overcome the child's impulsive nature. Immaturity is the tendency to act on what you feel over what you think or know. The path to adult maturity is the ability to think about what one should do and then acting on reason, rather than acting on feeling. Does this sound familiar? In the Bible, Paul writes of the struggle of knowing the right thing to do but being overcome with the desire to sin. No one questions the caring of a human dad when it comes to appropriate punishment and discipline. But when it comes to spiritual discipline, many lament at the moral lessons our Father sometimes forces us to learn in life. Because we regard ourselves as able to make our own decisions, we often have a tough time accepting the consequences of bad moral choices we make and often blame our Father for the consequences that follow. But, our Heavenly Father is there to help us recover from the bumps and setbacks we experience along our spirit journey.

One of the most overlooked traits in our Father is that He is very supportive of the things that we want to do in life. He endowed us with diverse personalities and gifts. In this great diversity, Father is engaged with us as individuals supporting each of us in achieving our spiritual goals in the context of real life experience. He cares about our education, our job, our relationships, and yes, even our heartaches. We have a Father that fully participates in every aspect of our lives as a Father should. Some of our concerns seem very small compared to the concerns of our Father as God. But, as His child, he takes special interest in the things that we are interested in so that we can develop the unique traits He placed in us. One day He hopes we can provide the same loving support to the people in need that we will inevitably encounter.

I am going to say something that few people understand. Our Father lets you make your mistakes. One of the most effective ways to gain learning and understanding is to experience the consequences of our actions. In the same way that an earthly dad understands that some lessons can only be learned through failure, our Father will let you experience the full measure of failure when you fail to learn the lessons He has been trying to teach you. Sometimes those lessons are very painful, and experiencing high levels of pain can confuse our view of Father. Believe me when I tell you that when you experience these terrible pains on the way to maturity, our

Father is experiencing those pains with you. I have often grieved at the pains my children were going through. Our Father is no different.

Our Father knows that none of us will be exactly like Him. Even Jesus was not exactly like Him. The Bible teaches that Jesus was made perfect through what he suffered and his reverent submission to the will of our Father, (Hebrews 5:7-10). If Jesus were exactly the same as God our Father, then he would have had nothing to submit to. There would have been no internal will that needed to submit to the will of our Father. Understand that our Father is not trying to make us into carbon copies of Himself. He is trying to help us be the best version of ourselves we can be. He has been trying to steer all people in the right direction since the creation birth.

All of the aspects that we recognize in a good earthly dad are mirrors of the Father we have in God. Good human dads are only reflecting our Father's ways when they excel as dads that are loved and admired by their families. Some dads instinctively know how to be dads because they are reflecting God in their spirits. That goes for motherly traits as well. Our Father being God reflects both the male and the female aspects of humanity.

Men And Women Reflect God's Image

In the creation story in the Bible, there is another passage that is often misread because for millennia people have been repeating a lie. The Bible does not say that God create man in His image. The Bible says that He created Mankind in His image. And the passage goes on to say male and female, He created them. What this means is that in creating Mankind, He separated the sides of His nature into male and female. Only the combined attributes of male and female together reflect the image of God. Although we commonly speak of God in His masculine attribute, none of us who know Father would deny that He also possess all the characteristics of a good mother as well.

Like dads, the number one trait of a mother is unconditional love, but mothers bring their own dimension to what that means. They bring a nurturing side. When we need that nurturing side, our Father fills that role fully. Like mom, our Father knows that He cannot be our friend if He is to be a parent. Mothers tend to deal with the messy side of parenting, and when things get confusing, messy, and emotional, you have a Father who is there with you to guide you to better days. Being a mother takes a great deal of patience. From the time a child is born, until the time a child moves out, children are constantly challenging the boundaries we set for them. Our Father put boundaries around us, and through our conscience, uses His voice to remind of what is right to lead us back to the right path continuously. When we run around like a child out of control, our Father is constantly using all the methods at His disposal to knock us back to a safer place without violating our right of free will.

I can tell you from personal experience that there were many days when I needed a mother, but in the middle of a large family there was not enough of my human mother to go around. I remember being in agonizing pain and tears with no one around to lend comfort. Those were the times when I opened myself up most to Father, and He came to comfort me. I could feel His love. I could feel the warm embrace of His arms. In these moments, I found and felt His comfort. I felt His nurture. I felt the calming voice of love telling me that I would be ok, and that I just needed to give myself time to heal and understand. I can close my eyes even now and remember the feeling of His strong presence in my time of emotional and physical need. But, as we know, a good parent/child relationship depends on trust and communication.

The Need For Trust

Children come into this world pretty helpless. It is months before we can eat solid food, and sometimes over a year before we can even walk. During that time, we accept our extreme dependence on our parents for our basic physical needs. By the time we learn to talk and express ideas, our time of helplessness established the trust bond that we form with our parents. In our spiritual walk, this trust bond can be more difficult to form because we often see ourselves as morally and mentally independent by the time we start to ponder our spiritual health. We often come to father with years of damaging experiences that make it very difficult to give anyone, let along God, blanket trust. But, if we are to grow spiritually, we have to work towards

Paul K. Lott, Sr.

that kind of blanket trust, the same kind of trust that a young child gives to a loving accepting parent.

In my experience, the number one obstacle to trusting our Father are the things we might have to give up if we gave Him that trust. Trusting in God our Father usually comes down to a list of all the stuff we don't want to stop doing. This is because we see our Father as God and not as a Father. We often see the judgment of God rather than the love of a Father. You can't help a child who does not trust you. Our Father cannot help you when you do not trust Him.

The most passionate proclamation that Jesus ever made was in defense of children. When he was out teaching, as he always did, and a group of children came to listen to him. His followers were annoyed and wanted the children to be taken away, but Jesus stopped them saying that unless adults came to him like a child, they could not enter the Kingdom of Heaven. He went on further to say the harshest statement he would make his entire ministry. He said that it was better to have a stone tied around one's neck and be thrown into he sea, than to bring harm to a child. Think of that. Jesus said that it would be better to be murdered by drowning then to face the consequences of bringing harm to a child. Children are trusting. They are open to new ideas. They are humble. The words of a trusted loving parent carry weight. It is this openness and trust that makes it possible for children to learn.

We see the result of broken trust in children. When a child grows up without a trusting relationship, it has terrible

51

effects on the child's ability to learn and grow. We often point to a child's lack of respect for authority as a central problem in schools and other places where children must engage with adults. In reality, a lack of trust in authority is rooted in the lack of a trusting relationship with a parent or close adult. That dysfunction manifests itself in a general lack of respect, and this lack of trust places serious obstacles in the child's life as they grow. Lack of trust in a parental relationship is the most serious roadblock to a child' future success. Why? Because a lack of trust impairs a child's ability to learn from a person in authority. If you don't accept a person's authority to teach you, you will not listen to what they have to say. In the same way, a lack of trust in our Father has the same result. If we don't give Him unconditional trust, chances are we will never learn the lessons He is trying to teach us. To learn from our Father, we must trust Him. The good news is that trust can be developed if we work to establish open communication with God the Father. We communicate with our Father through prayer.

Prayer And Communication

Talking to our Father should be such a simple act, yet many of the traditions we are taught in church have destroyed, rather than enhanced, our communication and relationship with the Father. The first tradition that harms our relationship with our Father is that most of us are taught not to pray to Him. Some pray to Jesus, others pray to 'saints', and while others recite prewritten prayers as their way of talking to Him. Jesus warned us about substituting our traditions for our Father's teaching. In the Bible (Mark 7:9) Jesus said, "You have a fine way of setting aside the commands of God in order to observe your own traditions!" The things listed above are traditions and go against Jesus's clear instructions.

This position on prayer comes from Jesus himself in the 'Lord's Prayer' (Bible passage Matthew 6:9) which begins, "This, then, is how you should pray: 'Our Father in Heaven, hallowed be your name, your kingdom come, your will be done, on Earth as it is in Heaven.'" The prayer begins with the words 'Our Father'. Our Father God sent Jesus to usher in a better relationship with Himself. Jesus always focused on bringing others into closer relationship to the Father. His ministry on Earth was to break the barriers to a strong relationship with our Father, and he never made an effort to bring others to worship him. People did, but people worship singers and movie stars as well. In fact, Jesus gave the Father credit for everything good about him (Bible passage Mark 10:18) he asked, "'Why do you call me good?" Jesus answered. "No one is good—except God alone." There is not a single scripture where Jesus asks anyone to pray to him. Jesus only asks us to pray to the Father in his name. When asked how to pray, Jesus first tells his followers that all prayer should be directed to the Father.

Our Father tries so hard to bring us closer to Him and to have a strong Father/Child relationship. It is heartbreaking to our Father to see the love He is seeking from each of us directed towards everyone but Him. The Bible teaches that God so loved that world the He (our Father) sent His only begotten Son, yet the Father rarely gets credit for the sending. Jesus prayed before his death for Father to spare him from torture and death. The reason Jesus followed through with our Father's plan was that Jesus was submitting himself to the Father's will. (Bible passage Matthew 26:39) This Jesus states. This Jesus affirms. Jesus ends with the bold declaration. "Yet not as I will, but as You will." It was Jesus's love for the Father that compelled him to give himself. On the cross, it was into our Father's hands that Jesus submitted his spirit in death. Father is the center of this story. All who have served have been in our Father's service, and that includes the Christ.

Prayer From the Heart

The second greatest tradition that harms one's relationship with Father is the reading of prayers. When I was very young, I wondered why people read prayers to the Father as their own. I couldn't imagine doing that to my mom or dad. It just never made sense to me. When I was in church with my family and the recited prayers started, I simply prayed my own prayer. They were not as elegant. I was only 6 or 7 years old, but I talked to Father about what was on my heart. Imagine if everyone in your life responded to your attempts at communication with a prewritten answer. I used to tell the story of the woman

54

who responded to her husband the same way many of us communicate with Father. Imagine a husband greeting his wife as she walks through the door from a busy day with "Hi honey. How was your day?" and the wife pulls a small book from her purse and reads, "How wondrous is my husband. How caring are his way." Or imagine the same thing happening with his children. Reading a response or a prayer to your Father is NOT prayer. Repeating the same memorized prayers to your Father is NOT communication. If prayer is communicating with the Father, then memorized or repetitious prayer does not qualify as real prayer.

I understand that memorized prayers are designed to make it easier to pray, but I need you to understand that memorized prayers result in you feeling good about a prayer that never actually happened. Our Father does not care to listen to the same prayers repeated by millions all over the globe. What He is interested in is genuine communication with His children. And like anything of value, effort is required. If we cannot fix communication with each other by speaking to each other in prewritten dialog, then we cannot fix our relationship with our Father using the same method. These practices have been taught for centuries without any support for these practices in the Bible text or from Christ himself. Jesus was clear that we are to focus our communication on the Father. After all, isn't being able to communicate directly with God, our Father, the whole point?

Jesus envisioned a day when people would feel free to talk with the Father wherever and whenever the urge existed. One of my favorite Bible stories is when Jesus encounters a woman at a well. After some brief conversation, the woman asks Jesus where is the proper place to worship. Jesus responds (Bible passage Matthew 4:23-24), "Yet a time is coming and has now come when the true worshipers will worship the Father in the Spirit and in truth, for they are the kind of worshipers the Father seeks. God is spirit, and his worshipers must worship in the Spirit and in truth." That time is now. Our Father does not live in statues or church buildings. Our Father lives with and in us. If we are to create a strong relationship with our Father, than it has to start with each of us reaching out to Him from the heart. Our Father is a parent seeking a relationship with His child. There are many powers in this universe; some are good and many are bad. But there is no greater power than two hearts expressing unconditional love: your Father loving you, and you loving Him in return.

Sometimes It Is Hard To Let Anyone In

So many people have told me that they don't know how to pray, or that they find it hard to open up to anyone, including Father. The truth is, He already knows what you need… and want… and He has already taken the first steps. He accepts you. He has sent servants in the form of people in your life to reach you in so many ways you may not know of. He has tried in so many ways to touch your life.

At times when you were unaware, He was there protecting you from what could have been worse. Father can't protect us from our bad decisions, or we would never learn to make better ones. And let me be clear, Father's will is not to see you harmed or hurt. It is His will to see you make your way back to Him. This is His ONLY goal for your life. When you hear others say that this bad thing or another was just God's will, don't believe them. It was your will. He had to let you make your mistakes so that you could develop into a child of Heavenly Character, full of goodness developed through struggle and humble temperament. Without a relationship directly with the Father, there is no Heaven for you. Go to church, do good deeds, help the poor, but without prayer, there is no way to come home to the Father of your soul...

The Revelare

Paul K. Lott, Sr.

Chapter Five
Significat Messiam

When I was a pastor, every year on Easter Sunday, I would preach a version of what I am about to share in these pages. The sermon was called "The Power of An Indestructible Life", and the point of the massage was to call attention away from the resurrection of Christ, and call attention back to the real meaning of Jesus's life. The first year, there was a bit of controversy. Many of my listeners took some time to understand why I felt the need to address their long held beliefs as a misunderstanding of the significance of Christ. After all, over the centuries, traditions have risen around the resurrection holiday. Most of those traditions have very little to do with why Christ was on that cross to begin with. Today, we focus on egg hunts and chocolate rabbits. Somewhere in there, we give a quiet nod to the resurrection story, but all we take away from the story is that Jesus paid the price for our sins and so we are free. While these practices seem harmless, they are not helpful, and are harmful because they distract us from the real story of Christ.

Jesus was not the first man crucified and he was not the last man crucified. Most people never come to realize that how Christ lived his life was more important than how he died. A crucified man is just a crucified man. A crucified man who lived a blameless life is a sacrifice. It was the kind of life Jesus lived that made his life indestructible. It was the life he lived and how he lived that makes all the difference for us.

Before Jesus lived, there was a problem. The problem had to do with our Father's standards, His laws and commands. How could anyone be condemned to live apart from Father if His standards were unreasonable? After all, can man be judged for not being able to do the impossible? Among those cast out of Heaven this was a powerful argument, but more importantly, this was a powerful excuse people and the Fallen gave themselves for the wrong they had done. "Nobody is perfect, so you can't judge me". Jesus was sent to address this myth. Another myth came after Jesus had lived, died, and risen from that death. This myth was that Jesus, as the Son of God, came to Earth with special powers that allowed him to live a perfect life, and that because he had this special power, he was given the added power of giving us a free pass from being accountable for our lives by requiring us to simply acknowledge him as Lord. The myth was that because he had this special power, ONLY he could live a perfect life and so we all are excused from trying too hard. After all, isn't sin just human nature?

No Special Powers

The first truth to understand is that in order for Jesus's life to have any meaning, he had to live his life without any special powers that are not also available to all of us as well. Because it was Mankind that needed the help, Jesus had to be completely human to demonstrate the solution. The Bible states this clearly (Hebrews 2:16-18), "For surely it is not angels he helps, but Abraham's descendants. For this reason he had to be made like them, fully human in every way, in order that he might become a merciful and faithful high priest in service to God, and that he might make atonement for the sins of the people. Because he himself suffered when he was tempted, he is able to help those who are being tempted."

What does it mean to be "fully human in every way"? It means that everything Jesus achieved had to be achieved through faith. If faith was to be the means by which we would learn to be as our Father wants us to be, then Jesus had to be restricted to this tool. Rather than a god walking through life showing us humans how it is done right, we have the image of a man exercising faith to achieve perfection. That means that Jesus learned through faith who he was. There is no indication that Mary ever talked to Jesus about the things that she witnessed during the time of his birth. Luke 2:19 records that "Mary treasured up all these things and pondered them in her heart." I don't think that Mary understood what the events meant to be able to talk intelligently to Jesus about them. Jesus had to look inside with prayer and meditation to discover his path. He lived 30 years before he even started his public ministry, presumably living the humble life of a carpenter like Joseph, his earthly dad. In those thirty years, Jesus experienced a full life and was faced with all of the questions we would face within our lives. The Bible says that he was tempted. That means that he encountered the opportunity and temptation to commit sin, but choose Father's path instead. Was he tempted to lie? Of course. Was he tempted with sexual sin? Of course. Was he tempted to abandon his Father's will to live a different path? Of course. But, as he walked through life, he learned from experience and built his faith on the principles of scripture. If we are to accept the Bible as the basis for our beliefs, then we must accept that Jesus came as a man identical to us in every way. He came as a man armed only with faith to guide him to his true mission in God. Through prayer and study, he discovered truth, He discovered who he was and what he was born to accomplish. He accepted the call of the Father and submitted his life and will to Him.

We know from scripture that Jesus struggled. Jesus learned. And that Jesus was made perfect through those struggles. The Bible makes this clear (Hebrews 5:7-8), "During the days of Jesus' life on Earth, he offered up prayers and petitions with fervent cries and tears to the one who could save him from death, and he was heard because of his reverent submission. Son though he was, he learned obedience from what he suffered and, once made perfect, he became the source of eternal salvation for all who obey him". Powerful words. The Bible teaches that even though he was the Son of God, he had to learn obedience during his time here on Earth. The cards were not stacked in his favor. Because the Bible says that he was heard because of his reverent submission to the Father, we know that he did not always understand or agree with what the Father wanted from him. The key to his power was that he reverently submitted himself despite his personal feelings as a human being. And it was in the process of living a submitted life to the Father that he was "made perfect". In other words, he became perfect as a human on this Earth. These are not my words, but an echo of the words written in the Bible, "once made perfect" from his suffering and submission. Jesus was very much like you and I. He very much struggled to be made perfect. His life is significant because he was able to live a life like us without committing sin against the Father.

The Bible does not teach that Jesus avoided sin with special powers from the Father or he walked the Earth as a god, immune to the world around him. He felt the pain, temptations, and struggles of this earthly life. Jesus did not have special schooling by angels to give him a leg up on avoiding sin. He read the scriptures and gleaned the insights he needed to understand his Father, and then through prayer, mediation, and communion with the Father, he grew as a person with a will accustomed to submission to his Father. He did not have flash backs to a time in Heaven when all of the problems of this life did not matter.

It was a life of faith. Jesus did not get secret teachings from his parents, rabbis, or Heavenly powers. Instead, he kept himself grounded in the spiritual tools of his time. And it was only through his faith that more truth was gradually revealed to him.

The power of an indestructible life cannot be found in recited prayers, magical Bible incantations, the doing of good deeds, or in the membership of a church. The power of an indestructible life can only be found through a heart that, though a relationship with the Father, submits to the teachings of that Father. The submission cannot be begrudgingly, but rather, that submission must be reverent. Reverent submission is willing submission. It is not a submission built on agreement or understanding. It is a submission based on a deeply trusting relationship directly with our Father. The life of Christ is our true example because his life demonstrates how we can be like him.

Be Perfect

The life of Christ teaches us our true potential as children of the Father. Jesus would never command us to do the impossible, right? Yet, the Bible records Jesus saying (Matthew 5:48), "Be perfect, therefore, as your Heavenly Father is perfect." One of the biggest myths we are taught to believe is that perfection is unachievable. If that is the case, then we have a Messiah who does not tell the truth. Jesus set before us in the Bible a realistic goal of moral perfection. What we have passed down to us, instead, is a myth of moral limitation. The process of being made perfect has nothing to do with always wanting to do the right things and doing it. The process of moral perfection is based on submitting to the will of the Father even when we don't agree or understand. In time, through our relationship with the Father, we gradually move towards the day when we reflect His will. The reflection of His perfect will is the definition of moral perfection.

I will tell you that this is not what you will hear from most religious leaders even though the Bible clearly states this truth. In scripture, over and over again, Jesus gives the command for us to stop sinning. Again, would he command us to do the impossible? When a person realizes that they have the power to never sin, it changes their life and perspective. No longer do we do wrong and proudly excuse ourselves with the words, "I am only human". In the Father's eyes, your humanity is a condition of higher potential. You are not governed by your passions and impulses, but instead, you are truly governed by your ability to submit to the will of the Father. To obey or not to obey is a matter of choice and not some uncontrollable aspect of evolution or biology. A human child grows to mental maturity by learning to ignore his/her impulses in favor of thoughtful action. Spiritual immaturity is the tendency to act impulsively on moral matters in favor of personal desires, rather than the will of our Father. Faith in the Father includes having faith in what He sees in you as a living soul. Faith in the Father means that we can no longer have faith in those who tell us that we are destined to always sin because "we are only human". Jesus was only human during his time on Earth. He is the example.

Unlearning thousands of years of human traditions and false beliefs is a difficult task. This is the reason we have a Helper. The Holy Spirit is that Helper. The Holy Spirit is not a possessing spirit that does all the work for us, however. I have heard it taught that once we truly have the Holy Spirit we won't want to do wrong. I think that misses the meaning of the word 'helper'. We do not become 'filled' with the Holy Spirit and then loose our free will. Christ sent the Holy Spirit as a helper. He would never send the Holy Spirit to make choices for you. In the end, Christ always intended for you to make the final decision. In the end, you are responsible. The Holy Spirit is there to remind you of the right choices at the moment of decision. Whether or not you follow them is entirely up to you. The Holy Spirit is a powerful advocate when we understand the purpose for the Holy Spirit in our lives.

The significance of the Messiah is that he showed all of us the way to perfection. The perfect life is a reflection of the Father in all that we do, not in all that we feel or think. The feeling and the thinking like our Father grows over time as we become more like our Father. Your biology or environment cannot negate this fact. The difference between success and failure on your spiritual walk will be the degree to which you choose to set aside your own impulsive will in favor of the Father's will.

The Death And Resurrection

So what importance does the death and resurrection have? Why is forgiveness so important? The answer lies in understanding the process of accountability and forgiveness in the human sense. When a child 'sins' against a parent, two things have to take place. First the child must accept the consequences of his/her actions. Second, the child must commit to change in a way that is acceptable to the parents. Otherwise, there is no incentive to change, learn, and grow. When a child 'sins' against his/her parent's wishes, there is a break of relationship. Not a destruction of the relationship, but a break. That break must be mended in order for the relationship to heal and continue along positive grounds. The child must do what the parent asks to mend those wounds to the relationship to re-establish trust. In the same way, when we sin against our Father, there is a break in the relationship because the act of sin constitutes a break in the trust between the Parent and Child. It is only when the child accepts his/her punishment and shows the will to be accountable that the trust can be healed. Sometimes the breaks are small. Sometimes the breaks are much larger. Until we come to know our Father, the break is immense, and frankly, there is not anything we can do to heal the break accept to be given grace. The sacrifice of the Christ is a tool to mead the breach by showing us the consequences of our actions. It makes us admit that what we do have consequences. The consequence was death. Spiritual death is defined as separation from the Father. Our Father must hold us to consequences for our own sake. Until we accept the weight of our actions, there can be no healing or change. In the same way, until our human children accept the weight of their actions there can be no healing of the parent/child relationship.

To allow for healing, the consequence can be suffered by an innocent volunteer - the Christ. Christ is the big brother who volunteered to take our punishment so that we would not have to suffer that punishment, and in doing so, erases the past so that we can start on a clean slate. But, it is only when we see and acknowledge that the punishment was just can we be free to change. If we don't feel we deserve punishment, we feel resentment towards the one bringing the punishment.

We need forgiveness because we know our offense towards the Father even before anyone tells us. When we lie, we know it is wrong. But we justify it to ourselves in other ways. When we use others for sexual pleasure or money, we know that it is wrong. Being wrong starts a kind of game that keeps us doing the same things. We repeat the wrong doing to convince ourselves that the wrong was not a wrong. We begin to reason that everyone is doing the same things so it is ok. I have never spoken to a person about God that has not had some issue with faith in the Father because of the changes they would have to make or the burden of having to admit their past wrongs. A person can get to the point where their identity is tied up in being a rebel. They mistake being entertained for happiness. I remember when maturity used to mean you denied your impulses to make better long-term choices. Today it means that you indulge all of your impulses as long as you are not hurting anyone. In truth, you are always hurting someone, starting with yourself. In truth, we have elevated grade school behavior (less the sex) and called it teenage behavior (with the sex). Teenage behavior (plus more sex) has become the new "adult" behavior. Truly growing up and developing a moral center is becoming more rare each day. With all of the garbage we come to the Father carrying, we need to undergo a formal process of forgiveness. This is so that we can let go of the past while we make an informed decision about changing our lives. Our relationship with the Father cannot be a casual relationship. It is an all or nothing relationship.

Christ showed us how to have a committed relationship with the Father throughout our lives, and he facilitated the process that makes it possible for you to first face the past and then let go of the past. We call it grace when a parent lets us out of a punishment we deserve. Our Father gives us grace on the condition that we work with Him toward permanent change. Any parent would expect this. If we can accept what Christ has done on our behalf, our Father is willing to let our past disobedience go. Father does not offer us a contractual relationship. He is not just making an arrangement. A better way to understand it would be as if you had an older sibling named Tommy, and when you refused to clean your room, your brother Tommy did it for you. Now the room is clean so your parents come to you and say that you will avoid punishment as long as you accept Tommy's example and agree to live by Tommy's example. The option of grace is free because it is unearned. But that does not mean there is not an obligation tied to the acceptance of that grace. Remember the days when banks offered a free toaster if you opened an account? You couldn't buy the toaster because the toaster was free, but you still had to open an account to get it. The purpose of forgiveness is to enable an intimate relationship with the Father using Christ as the example of how to do that. Forgiveness is not some 'gift' given without obligation attached. If you accept the gift, you accept the Father and all the responsibilities that come with being a family member.

Chapter Six
Ecclesia

Jesus came with a purpose, and that purpose was to facilitate a direct relationship between a Father and His Children. It was a mission of love to bridge the gap between Mankind and God. The plan was a simple one: forgiveness in return for a commitment to the Father. To Jesus, this was never a religious issue. It was a family issue. During his time on Earth, Jesus continuously faced religious traditionalism as the biggest obstacle to his message. Religious traditionalism is the greatest obstacle of the Christian faith and must be destroyed if we are to live lives dedicated to the Father.

Religious Traditionalism

Religious traditionalism is the enshrinement of faith under a religious veil of ceremony and rituals that remove the believer from the intended object of their faith - our Heavenly Father. Faith is a simple idea. Putting true faith in the Father results in the believer living a life in tune with that faith relationship. Religious traditionalism distracts God seekers from developing true faith by inserting rituals, ceremonies, organizational structures, and church traditions into the life of the seeker. Seekers spend more time trying to understand and practice traditions rather than actually practicing faith and developing a relationship with the Father.

Organized opposition to the teaching of Christ came from those who were dedicated to their religious traditions - the religious leaders of Jesus's day. Two groups, one called Pharisees and another Sadducees, devoted themselves to opposing Jesus at every opportunity. Jesus rejected religious traditions in favor of living according to faith principles. These religious leaders had developed their particular traditions on how to be a Jew and created an organizational structure around those traditions. These traditions layered requirements on top of what was already written in the scriptures. Where the Bible commanded men to rest on the Sabbath day, the religious traditionalist listed out rules about what 'resting' meant. You could not help another person, but you could get your livestock out of a ditch. You could not walk more than so many steps or it was considered work. Hands needed to be washed in a particular way. There were rules on when to pray and how to pray, etc.

When a person focuses on traditions and rituals, they loose focus on the Father. We already talked about prayer traditions like reading prayers, praying to others rather than the Father, etc. All of these prayer practices are traditions created by men. Jesus was clear on who we should pray to. Jesus was asked directly how to pray and responded that our prayers are to be directly addressed to our Father. Jesus made a clear statement that is not subject to interpretation. Jesus warned that religious traditions would destroy our faith. (Bible passage Mark 7:9), "You have a fine way of setting aside the commands of God in order to observe your own traditions!" Adding traditions onto what is clearly instructed in the Bible is setting aside the commands of the Father to observe a human tradition.

Many would be surprised that Jesus never intended to start a new religion. Jesus was trying to cut trough all the religious distractions to offer a more simple, pure relationship with the Father. His fight was against the religious leaders of the day and their traditions that only led to loyalty to the religious authority and not to the truth of the Father. Most religious leaders are very sincere. They all began as God seekers looking to serve the Father and help others find the path to God. We go to a church and become part of a group, but in the end, our focus is the traditions of the organization. Even when a young seeker reads obvious contradictions to Biblical teaching, they let those contradictions be explained away because they are now a part of the group and so are driven to conform to that group's traditions. I want to go through some examples to make this point clear.

Calling a Man, Father

The Bible: Matthew 23:9, And do not call anyone on Earth 'father,' for you have one Father, and he is in Heaven.

The Tradition: Many church groups have priests and ministers whom are taught to be called 'father' or even 'holy father'.

The Harm: The command is ignored, teaching believers that it is ok to ignore what is written in favor of the contradictions a person teaches you. The respect as father that is due only to God the Father is now shared with a human authority. The meaning of God as Father is completely lost in the practice.

Praying to Jesus and "Saints"

The Bible: Matthew 6:9-13, "This, then, is how you should pray: 'Our Father in Heaven...'

The Tradition: Most church groups instruct believers to pray to Jesus. Jesus never asked this to be done. He only asked that prayer be in his name. Other groups go as far as to instruct its followers to address their prayers to past believers with the special title of 'saint'.

The Harm: The direct focus of our spiritual relationship is no longer God alone. Communication that belongs to the Father is now divided among others with no right to that communication. The purpose of Christ to bring us into a direct relationship the Father is undermined.

Paul K. Lott, Sr.

Unmarried Church Bishops (Elders) Without Families

<u>The Bible:</u> 1 Timothy 3:5, "If anyone does not know how to manage his own family, how can he take care of God's church?"

<u>The Tradition:</u> Requiring Bishops and all church leaders to be single and celibate.

<u>The Harm:</u> Placing the sole requirement for leadership on the character of a man in a family means that the Father knows there are traits and lessons that can only he learned as part of a family. The intangible lessons learned leading a family are the lessons the Father designated as the most important knowledge needed to lead a church. The center of the faith was meant to be the biological family. In the context of the biological family, believers learn the unwritten lessons of the faith, and have a place to practice the core values of the faith in a trusted environment. God did not place a theology education requirement, a preaching ability requirement, or even a teaching requirement (though the Bible teaches that the ability to teach would be a nice add-on). The lack of family centered leadership has created a system that is unable to excel at the Father's primary goal of creating a church community that is based on the principles of the family.

Appointing a Single Bishop (Elders) Over Large Territories

The Bible: Titus 1:5 "...appoint elders (Bishops) in every town, as I directed you."

The Tradition: Appoint a single Bishop to lead large territories.

The Harm: Church leadership was never intended to be based on the leadership of a single person. Preaching, teaching, and evangelizing are gift-based activities. Church leadership is a character-based activity. This is why a spiritual gift was not listed as a requirement to lead a community of families. To protect against a human hierarchy of authority, elders (Bishops) were appointed in number. Leadership was by consensus of a group bishops on a city-by-city basis. Church leadership was to be a single layer of equals above the community, not a hierarchy of authority.

Forbidding People To Marry

The Bible: 1 Timothy 4:1-3, "The Spirit clearly says that in later times some will abandon the faith and follow deceiving spirits and things taught by demons. Such teachings come through hypocritical liars, whose consciences have been seared as with a hot iron. They forbid people to marry..."

The Tradition: In order to be devoted to God, one must remain single and follow the rules of a church.

The Harm: This practice goes against the teaching on church leadership and adds rules that Christ never intended. Elevating the place of single, celibate believers above those taking part in a family, where God wanted the emphasis, is a reversal of the Father's intent. The Bible teaches, "So God created mankind in his own image, in the image of God he created them; male and female he created them.(Genesis 1:27). The only true reflection of God's character is in the merging of male and female personalities. A man and a woman together reflect the image of God, not as separate persons.

Faith vs. Works

The Bible: James 2:18-19, "But someone will say, "You have faith; I have deeds. Show me your faith without deeds, and I will show you my faith by my deeds. You believe that there is one God. Good! Even the demons believe that—and shudder."

The Tradition: Salvation is a free gift. Belief does not require change.

The Harm: The teaching that works are not apart of the Christian faith creates a group of believers who are convinced that being a better person is optional in the practice of the faith. The false idea was so wide spread even in the early days of the church that James had to write a letter to address the false teaching specifically. Jesus taught lesson in 48 parables in the Bible. The outcomes of all 48 parables were based on the actions taken. True faith always results in better actions.

The Growing Number of Denominations

<u>The Bible:</u> 1 Corinthians 1:10, "I appeal to you, brothers and sisters, in the name of our Lord Jesus Christ, that all of you agree with one another in what you say and that there be no divisions among you, but that you be perfectly united in mind and thought.

<u>The Tradition:</u>   Methodist, Baptist, Catholics, Lutherans, Church of Christ, plus 100s more.

<u>The Harm:</u> The faith is divided and the churches spend more time in conflict and conversation with each other, than in doing the real work of the Father.   The word 'denomination' means 'of names'. The expanded passage in 1 Corinthians specifically ban Christians dividing into named camps.   Named Christian communities must emphasis their traditions to differentiate themselves to attract converts to their camp, but these converts are converts to a church group and not to our Father.

Child Baptism

<u>The Bible:</u> Acts 2:38, Peter replied, "Repent and be baptized, every one of you, in the name of Jesus Christ for the forgiveness of your sins. And you will receive the gift of the Holy Spirit.

<u>The Tradition:</u> Baptizing babies and children, ignoring that repenting is required before baptism. Since a baby or child cannot repent, they cannot be baptized. Baptizing for sins 'born' into a child is a fabricated tradition that has

nothing to do with the intent of adult baptism. The tradition of 'confirmation' is also a fabricated tradition.

The Harm: Adults no longer feel the burden to make an informed decision to follow Christ. The perception has emerged that people are 'born' into a particular religious group, rather than converted to follow the example of the Christ. This practice weakens the entire church community by creating a community called Christians who never actually repented of their past sins or having committed themselves to live as Christ lived. These communities are not real Christian communities.

I could list a dozen more instances where traditions have replaced the teachings of Christ and the Apostles. Some things do a little harm. Other things deeply harm the faith. All religious traditions arise for the same reason. God sends a prophet to reveal another part of His truth to mankind. During the immediate life of that prophet, the message is heard, understood and acted upon. Once the prophet dies, others step into try to fill in the "gaps" they think have been left by the prophet. These men try to expand on the "how" and loose track of the "what and why". Soon, what is left are a set of traditional practices that are devoid of the original message. Within a single generation the original intent is forgotten or abandoned.

Religious traditionalism damages the church Christ intended to leave behind. Religious Traditionalism undermines the very fabric of the Father's intent. It leaves families without needed spiritual resources and leaves the church unable to transform society. I grieve to say it, but I absolutely believe that there is very little of what Christ intended left in the churches of today. When I say "church" I mean all flavors of the church as they exists across the planet. What we have today is not what God intended. It is not what is described in the scriptures. It does not follow Christ's intent or command. It does not reflect the understanding or intent of the original Apostles. Each Sunday, millions of people meet to hear a sermon, take communion, give a contribution, read some prayers or have prayers read to them, and then they quietly go home with the satisfaction that they have "paid their respects" to God. When I witness this, all I think are the words of Isaiah, "…but their hearts are far from me…" Every Sunday individuals show up at church and then return to their individual lives. Church is seen as a service organization for the benefit of its individual members and not as a family of servants gathered for the benefit of extending the Father's love to the lost and broken.

I believe that most people who regularly go to church started doing so because they truly wanted to seek a greater understanding of God. I use the words "understanding of God" to mean that most people never really make a big effort to get to "know" Him directly. They seek only to find out more "about" God. Churches evolved providing this information "about" God. Church services are basically lecture halls. One person stands in front of a group of people and provides "information". The process is not unlike what happens in college lecture halls everyday. The only difference with the church is that homework is optional. Even the Sunday school and Bible study formats are not very different from church services except attendees can ask questions. The reading of prayers and the emphasis on rituals stops most people from ever knowing God although they certainly are learning more about God. People leave church "feeling" holy without ever really doing anything. They leave the church feeling "cleansed". The act of paying respects to God is all that is needed by most people to feel better about themselves.

True Worship

The idea of a "worship" service is a fabricated tradition. The scriptures do call for believers to meet, but we were never told to do this for the purpose of worship. In scripture, there is no such thing as a worship service. Worship is not fundamentally a group activity in the scriptures, but rather the spontaneous outpouring of adoration for the Father by individuals, usually in response to witnessing or experience of an act of the Father. Genuine worship is a response to something experienced. When a person sees the hand of the Father working in his/her life, and spontaneously praises Him by expressing gratitude, that is genuine worship. When a person stands in a group of people reading prayers written by other people, or simply bowing ones head to a long well spoken prayer recited by a priest or pastor, this is not anything close to worship. This is closer to theatre than worship. Yes, the emotions may be real, but a good movie can create real emotions. That does not make the movie real life.

There is a passage in the Book of Deuteronomy in the Bible that reads, "You shall surely destroy all the places where the nations whom you shall dispossess served their gods, on the high mountains and on the hills and under every green tree. You shall tear down their altars and dash in pieces their pillars and burn their Asherim (objects related to worshipping a god) with fire. You shall chop down the carved images of their gods and destroy their name out of that place. You shall not worship the Lord your God in that way." God wants us to worship Him is a way that is real. The pagan gods received artificial worship because they were not real people. Our Father is a real person. He directed us not to place Him in the same mold as gods made of statues and relics, and worshipped with rituals. Yet, despite His express command not to worship Him that way, most Christians worship Him that way.

God gave into David reluctantly over the building of a Temple. God never wanted a Temple because He knew that people would forget what actual worship was, and would start to "worship" like the pagan cultures they witnessed. Around that Temple would emerge traditions that would distance the people from their Father. By the time of Christ, what do we witness in the Bible? We witness a religious leadership heavily reliant on traditions. We witness the rise of religious traditionalism in the faith.

We go to special buildings we now call churches, when churches are supposed to be groups of people apart from a building. We even insult God by calling these buildings "the house of God" and by assigning them sacred status. We bow to relics and pray to statues of 'saints'. Pastors and priests administer "sacraments" such as communion as "magic" rituals. God made all water, yet we are convinced that some water has "magic" and we call this "magical" water "holy water". In the pagan past, people wore special clothes to go to their Temples, and we duplicate this same practice today by dressing up for "church" to show God our "best" (as if the homeless guy who we call Christ would really be that interested in seeing you dressed in your "best" for Him). Finally, Christ never asked that we pray to dead "saints". He never said to erect statues or pray to them. He explicitly stated that we are not to worship Him in this way, and yet Christians have adopted the traditions of the early pagan religions as their own. We hide from our Father in a sea of traditions that invoke emotion but produce little change in our character and even less of a relationship with the Father.

Once the Jerusalem church was destroyed, organized Christianity was mostly spread among the gentile or pagan converts. Churches began to adopt the pagan practices and understanding of Christian beliefs within the confines of their past pagan experiences. The Emperor Constantine was a sun worshipper and it was he that mostly led the followers of Christ to adopt pagan methods of worship. After making Christianity legal, Constantine erected meeting halls designed after the pagan practices he understood and so continued the church's downfall into pagan practices rebranded as Christian practices. God never intended for believers to gather in large groups for a 'worship' service. You were never intended to gather at a church building each Sunday to hear a sermon, have prayers read, give a contribution, and then return to an outside life. The Bible never commands you to attend church, as you understand it, or a 'worship' service. The Bible does command groups of believers to meet together, but not for the purpose of a 'worship' service or a sermon. They were to gather for fellowship (spiritual communication).

In the Bible passages recorded in 1 Corinthians 11 says, "When you come together, it is not the Lord's supper that you eat. For in eating, each one goes ahead with his own meal. One goes hungry, another gets drunk. What! Do you not have houses to eat and drink in? Or do you despise the church of God and humiliate those who have nothing? What shall I say to you? Shall I commend you in this? No, I will not. For I received from the Lord what I also delivered to you, that the Lord Jesus on the night when he was betrayed took bread, and when he had given thanks, he broke it, and said, "This is my body which is for you. Do this in remembrance of me." In the same way also he took the cup, after supper, saying, "This cup is the new covenant in my blood. Do this, as often as you drink it, in remembrance of me." For as often as you eat this bread and drink the cup, you proclaim the Lord's death until he comes. ... So then, my brothers, when you come together to eat, wait for one another— if anyone is hungry, let him eat at home—so that when you come together it will not be for judgment."

In this passage, Paul is clearly talking about "church services" as a common meal, where part of which, wine and bread are passed to remember Christ. He is not describing a worship services and he (nor anyone else for that matter) is not describing the lecture style meetings that we accept as church today. Even today, most people understand the importance of the family meal as a time for families to stay connected. There are many studies that have demonstrated the positive effect of sharing a common meal as a family. The primary way that people interact in general is over a meal. Friends meet for lunch. Dating most often takes place over a meal. Whenever someone talks about "going out" it usually involves a meal. Meals are intimate activities. Meals allow for free flowing conversation and genuine opportunities to get to know someone. This was the original setting for the church. The church began as a group of believers whose primary time of fellowship was in the taking of a common meal. During that meal, the taking of the wine and bread was added in obedience to Christ's command. The Lord's Supper as a Common Meal should be the primary activity of the churches. I am sure that most people reading this will find it obvious why the common meal provide more of a forum for learning, forming new relationships, and seeking relevant spiritual knowledge.

Paul's first letter to the Corinthians teaches that we are to gather to "let all things be done for building up". Rather than hearing a pastor's sermon and a beautiful choir, we are told that members of the group are to "share a lesson, a hymn, a revelation, a tongue, or an interpretation". Again, this goes against what is done in churches today. Encouragement is not to come from the pulpit, but from the people. Sermons get people too focused on Bible facts and matters of doctrine. When people share a meal, they tend to talk about what is relevant and personal. Women have the opportunity to share with other women the issues they face in practicing their faith as mothers, workers, daughters, and as friends. Men often experience a different kind of stress for different reasons, and the Lord's Supper would give these men an equal chance to explore questions of faith. Couples would hear from other couples. Children would be able to interact with other children in a common setting. The Lord's Supper as a common meal is how it was intended to be.

What Father wants you to do is to gather with other believers at regular intervals to encourage one another, and to share insights and questions about your spiritual walk over a meal. Church meetings were intended to be times of fellowship and two-way communications. Each of the members of the meeting comes ready to share. We know that personal growth only comes from real communication between people. We would never try to raise children by sitting them down periodically like churches do these days. They might sit there out of respect, but the relationship wouldn't go very far. Why would you think that our Father would want to "raise" you this way? Everyone understands the importance of shared meals in our biological families. They are the times when we bond with our children and the best opportunity for keeping in touch as a family unit. It would seem this effective method for family unity and growth would be the means by which our Father builds His Church.

Church meetings were designed to involve more people in participation, and we know that it was to be an open place to ask spiritual questions. Group members encourage one another by sharing their lessons and experiences within the context of their common belief. Anyone should be able to share a lesson or testimony. While the role of choirs in groups meetings should be abolished, members can still come together to create music of encouragement and share that with the group. While preachers will still preach, in our meetings, it is more important that there be teaching, and questions answer and explored. We know that teaching, and not preaching, was to be the preferred activity within the church. Preaching is mostly for "outsiders" while teaching is for those committed to being a part of the church body. The primary role of the pastor should be as a group facilitator, and not preacher. He should be an organizer whose goal is to get as broad participation as possible from those he shepherds. A pastor guides a flock. This means that he guides them to ACTION and a common understanding through action. This is a harder job, but it is the job pastors were intended to be doing. Pastor and preacher are NOT supposed to be the same thing. Pastors were never intended to act as priest. He was never intended to stand between our Father and His children. He was intended to be the older brother who helps keep the family healthy through communication and charitable action as an expression of growing character. At the meetings of the church, as many people as possible should be leading prayers, teaching lessons, and sharing testimonies. The pastor's job is to help the members grow in these activities of spiritual expression. People tend to work harder to understand things better when they have to say them in front of other people. Pastors should be focused more on training the trainer, rather than doing everything while the members just watch... In reality, people are tired of watching, and that is why church attendance has suffered. The kind of church I am speaking of is always relevant to the members because they learn through involvement.

While for special occasions a church community may choose to come together in large groups, the church should always meet in small groups so that as many people as possible have an opportunity to participate. Father never intended for mega churches to exist the way they exist today. He never intended for thousands of people to spend the bulk of their spiritual meetings listening to one man talking every Sunday. Listening is not doing. In such large groups, people tend to hide and not grow. If the goal is for spiritual growth, than there is no place for the mega church. There is no place for the large auditoriums. There is no place for spending all that money on buildings and building maintenance. Within every mega church there are hundreds of potential servants hiding in the crowd and never answering God's call to speak...to facilitate the participation of others in the group experience. If you follow a Master who was essentially a homeless man, there is no justification for spending thousands or millions of dollars on buildings and decorations. A nice setting attracts lots of people, but what you want is to attract the right people... people who are attracted by the good things your church DOES to serve others. You don't want people who are only attracted by the sound system and comfortable chairs. This is what our Father expects of you. Your tool of ministry should be kindness to those less fortunate, and not by the charisma of your speaking.

The church structure that we have inherited today is about control. The church "fathers" after the death of the apostles and the destruction of the Jerusalem church were more concerned about controlling doctrine. Wrongly, they reacted to false teachings being spread in such a way that the personal spiritual growth of each member became secondary to controlling the message. The Jerusalem church was largely vested in the authority of witness. A group of men shared 3 years of their lives with the Messiah and were transformed by that experience. In response, they spread the story of the amazing life they witnessed and the powerful message of forgiveness and redemption. Jesus had for all time taken the doctrine of judgment and guilt off the table... and instead gave us a new way of life rooted in caring for those less fortunate, personal morality, and eternal mercy. This is not the church that survives today.

The Purpose of Preaching

You won't find an example of our modern worship style anywhere in the scriptures. In all of the examples where we see preaching, that preaching is done to groups of unbelievers. Jesus' sermon on the mount and other sermons were all spoken to gathering crowds that were following the His message, but are not part of his circle. He moved from city to city spreading His reform message. When he spoke with the disciples for the purpose of teaching, it was a two way communication where the inner circle was allowed to ask questions, either about some teaching he had given them in private or about some preaching they witnessed him deliver to the unbelieving crowd.

John the Baptist preached (declared) a message to win followers to that message. Jesus preached (public speaking) to crowds to declare his message. There are dozens of passages that show preaching to be a public activity done to win others to the message. There is not a single passage of scripture where preaching is used for the edification of the believing. Believers' hearing the preaching resigned to a private setting to be taught the meaning of what was preached. Paul stated in dozens of passages that people came to belief through preaching, but within the assembly of the saints, preaching was never spoken of or commanded. The scriptures bear this out when the Apostles contrast the preaching of the Gospel to unbelievers with service within the assembly of the saints. In the Book of Acts (Acts 6:1-4) it reads:

"Now in these days when the disciples were increasing in number, a complaint by the Hellenists arose against the Hebrews because their widows were being neglected in the daily distribution. And the twelve summoned the full number of the disciples and said, "It is not right that we should give up preaching the word of God to serve tables. Therefore, brothers, pick out from among you seven men of good repute, full of the Spirit and of wisdom, whom we will appoint to this duty. But we will devote ourselves to prayer and to the ministry of the word." And what they said pleased the whole gathering, and they chose Stephen, a man full of faith and of the Holy Spirit, and Philip, and Prochorus, and Nicanor, and Timon, and Parmenas, and Nicolaus, a proselyte of Antioch. These they set before the apostles, and they prayed and laid their hands on them."

Peter even delivered the famous sermon on the day of Pentecost to an unbelieving crowd. We don't have any account of this type of preaching continuing within the assembly of the saints.

Order In the Meeting of the Saints

Revisiting Paul's first letter to the Corinthians, (1 Corinthians 14:26-32) it reads:

"What then, brothers? When you come together, each one has a hymn, a lesson, a revelation, a tongue, or an interpretation. Let all things be done for building up. If any speak in a tongue, let there be only two or at most three, and each in turn, and let someone interpret. But if there is no one to interpret, let each of them keep silent in church and speak to himself and to God. Let two or three prophets speak, and let the others weigh what is said. If a revelation is made to another sitting there, let the first be silent. For you can all prophesy one by one, so that all may learn and all be encouraged, and the spirits of prophets are subject to prophets. For God is not a God of confusion but of peace."

The passage starts with the instruction, "each one has a hymn, a lesson, a revelation, a tongue, or an interpretation." This passage tells us who should be doing the speaking - the general population. Paul only places a limit as to the number of speakers to being only two or three in turn. Nowhere does he speak of a sermon of any kind. Then he goes on to limit the number of those who prophesy to two or three. Now prophesy in scripture has nothing to do with predicting the future, or being recognized on the level of the great prophets of the scripture. Prophesying means to literally speak on behalf of God according to the message given to you by Father's Spirit. This is different from an interpretation where you are sharing an interpretation of a particular passage of scripture.

Paul continues (verses 34 - 35), "As in all the churches of the saints, the women should keep silent in the churches. For they are not permitted to speak, but should be in submission, as the Law also says. If there is anything they desire to learn, let them ask their husbands at home. For it is shameful for a woman to speak in church."

This passage might offend the sensitivities of the women who read it but we need to look a little further to understand its meaning. First, this command is limited to the married women. The reason is not that women are inferior, but rather, in the instance of married women, the provision is made for the sake of the spiritual condition of the marriage. Married women ask the question to their husbands. If the husband cannot answer, he presents the question to the assembly so that the couple learns and grows together. Married couples have one spiritual life before the Father. In private, they are to explore their spiritual growth together. By one of them presenting the question for the couple, they both learn and explore together with the husband as the spokesman for the couple in these matters. We know that many societies are male dominant. The scriptures don't seek social reform, but rather, seeks spiritual growth in the context of the larger human society. I would add that families take the same approach in general. It is not unlike a family talking over issue during dinner, and than one of them seeking answers for the group in the public forum for the sake of the gathering being orderly. In many settings that contain groups of people, the group spokesman speaks on behalf of the group. So it should be in the meeting of the saints.

A word on the roles that the scriptures outline. Roles are a way of organizing groups of people. Roles establish order to accomplish a purpose. Because a woman is asked to play a role, does not make her inferior. It is merely the division of responsibility within a marriage. The bible seeks to free women for their other purposes within the family unit by dividing marital responsibilities.

Our renewed church must follow these principles. I know many will argue that the way the current church conducts services is not harmful and has helped people in many ways. I would agree that it has done some good, but as we can see today, churches are emptying out. If we are bold enough to renew the original intent of the assembly of the saints, then the church will be renewed in both purpose and effectiveness. Abolish the way you worship in the churches through "worship" services. Go back to the beginning. As a church, meet together for the common meal, and pass the bread and wine in remembrance. After you have eaten, let the individual members of the assembly offer hymn, lessons, tongues, revelations, and prophesy. Give each member the opportunity to share their personal faith experiences, and ask the questions they need to grow and understand. Do this as a family of believers.

True worship is a form of prayer. True worship takes place when an individual expresses their adoration, gratitude, and love towards the Father. True worship takes place any time and any place. True worship takes place when the need strikes an individual to worship and praise. It emerges from one's personal relationship with our Father. Our Messiah tells us that our bodies are the temples of God, and it is in the heart that true worship takes place. Father finds the church's obsession with buildings detestable. This practice has taught people to feel holiness within a building rather than where they should feel the Holiness of God, within their very own hearts. The kingdom of Heaven is within. Buildings have no meaning.

Our Father created the church as a community for believers. The rules of the church are much the same as the rules of a family. Growth and learning in a church is based on communication with the Father and with each other. The church can only be healthy when communication flows like blood in the body. When circulation stops, the body becomes sick. When I say I love the church, I am mean that I love when the children of the Father come together as a family community. Make your church into a healthy family and everyone will grow in their walk with the Father. Religious traditionalism will always fight back and defend the status quo. Change can come, but we must be committed to change.

The Revelare

Chapter Seven
Familia

The family is the foundation of humanity. Setting aside religious belief entirely, this is true across all societies and across all cultures. Every family starts with a man and a woman. This is true no matter what a family looks like in the end, because it always takes a man and a woman to conceive a child. Even science cannot take the egg of a woman and the seed of a man out of the making of a baby.

Continuing to set religion aside, much has been made of organic foods. The idea being that we need to get rid of all artificial ingredients and return to doing things the natural way. Natural is better, right? So, I am advocating the organic family, the family that occurs in nature when all of the artificial ingredients are taken out. The organic family is the basis of human life and society. The organic family is one man and one woman forming a partnership to live a life and raise their offspring together. They build their home life together. They have children, and together, care for their children to prepare them for the day when their children will create their own families. Couples having children and their children having children are what society is built upon. In a natural society, an organic society, culture emerges to support the creation of families.

Because the family starts with a man and a woman, our Father places a very special emphasis on the relationship between a man and a woman. The Bible teaches that when a man and a woman join sexually, they become one body. When a man and a woman join in marriage, they become one person in the eyes of the Father. They live a joined spiritual life. I have talked about the creation of man before and emphasized that God's image is reflected in the joint personalities of man and woman together. Our Father is both protector and nurturer. He has the traits of both sexes. We are drawn to find a mate for more than sexual reasons. We are drawn to find a mate for spiritual growth and emotional fulfillment. A healthy marriage is a safe haven of emotional acceptance and expression. The sexual dynamic within a marriage creates greater emotional openness.

It was never intended that marriage relationships be temporary in nature. Society has come to accept divorce as the norm, but our Father continues to teach that divorce is a disease. I remember when I first read Jesus's statement that divorce did not always exist, but that Moses allowed it in his law because of the stubbornness of man. I did a quick check of the Bible and found, to my surprise, that divorce was never mentioned until the law of Moses. Marriage was permanent. Even separated couples were still considered to be husband and wife. I believe that when it is generally accepted that marriage is a permanent act, men, women, and their families are more careful in mate selection. Marriage is not centered on love alone. It has to be based on more than love. A good relationship ultimately produces love, respect, trust, and a stable environment to raise children. A bad relationship ultimately results in a withdrawal of respect, trust, and then finally, love.

When I worked as a full time pastor in a church in Pennsylvania, the number one reason couples told me they wanted to get married was that they were in love and wanted to spend the rest of their lives together. Imagine their surprise when I told them that I didn't think that was a very good reason. My marriage counseling revolved around helping the couple take a closer look at each other. If matters of character were addressed, then I moved forward. I have never supported what I felt would obviously be a bad relationship. The signs are easy to spot.

Why Love Alone Is Not Enough

Early love is based, at least in part, on a person we have imagined. Because we are hopeful or have feelings for a person, we endow them with virtues and strengths that we have never witnessed in their character. Any feelings of love you may have for a person quickly fades when you discover poor character in them, or you find that you do not want the same kind of life. Everyone has flaws, even Christians, but we often overlook the flaws of a fellow believer. We make wrong assumptions about their character and suitability as a spouse.

Because you don't see the whole person at first, that person gets a chance to present to you the person they want you to believe they are. It may even be the person they want to be. Christians in particular have a drive to present their best Christian face. Everyone presents his or her best side when dating. (Well, everyone who wants a second date). This means that the person you may find yourself drawn to may not really be the person you are with. In time, the real person comes out, but in many cases, you may already feel an emotional bond, and so continue to date a person even when there are clear signs that you may not be with the right person. You begin to overlook flaws that damage the relationship, holding on to the notion that he/she will change for the better given enough time. I can say that I have seen many relationships that continue because one person is hoping for the other to improve, and so, constantly make excuses for the other person's bad behavior or lack of character.

I don't advocate that Christians only date with the mindset of getting married. What I do advocate is that dating be used to develop the ability to know how to evaluate a person's moral character and value system. It is a learning process that takes some practice. You have to go into dating with the mindset of ending the relationship quickly if you see that the person you are dating does not have the character to build a strong healthy long-term relationship.

Essential Things To Look For

You should determine if you share a common purpose with the person you are dating. Many people are attracted to each other because they have a lot of superficial things in common. Having things in common is not the same thing as sharing a common purpose. You may both be Christians and like the same music, movies, or share of a love of dining. But, if you are together for 30 years or more, those common activities will get old. I mean, if you both love tennis, how many games of tennis are you going to share before it is no longer enough to carry the relationship? You need a common purpose. You need to find someone with the same view of what life is about. Even among Christians, you will find great variation on what a common purpose means. Some Christians focus on family, while others focus on ministry or service. Make sure that your purpose matches with your potential partner. You will be spending a lot of time together. Make sure you both want to be doing the same things driven by a common purpose. You can either grow together in a marriage, or grow apart. At least 50% of those in marriages grow apart. That is why it is critical to choose someone who lives for the same purpose. A common purpose keeps you growing in the same direction.

Be certain that you want the same kind of relationship as your prospect. In all my years of marriage counseling, I have seen many good and sincere couples in a marriage where each person wanted a different kind of relationship entirely. Some people want a marriage that is centered on the relationship itself. Work, children, and other activities are secondary to spending as much time as possible with each other. I have also known people who want a 'check in' relationship where each pursues their job or career and are very happy coming together from largely separate lives to spend a little time together. In most of my counseling situations, one person wants the relationship to be at its center, while their spouse is perfectly happy just checking in. These are two extreme examples, and there are a lot of other types of relationships in between. I guarantee that there will be conflict when you don't want the same kind of marriage as your spouse, so make sure the type of relationship you want matches your prospect's before you develop feelings at all.

It is critical to select a person who accepts you as you are and not for someone they hope you to become. I define emotional abuse as being in an intimate relationship with someone you don't completely accept. Even if you try to hide it, your lack of acceptance will come out in your behavior, and your partner will know by your attitude and words. Your partner will become afraid to express their feelings, communication will suffer severely, and trust will be lost. A person who is not accepted for who they are tends to start lying a lot in an attempt to present a pleasing image. The relationship will spiral to pieces. No one should ever be punished for expressing their feelings, even the silliest of feelings. All relationship should be a place of emotional safety. That means that you should be able to express yourself freely at all times and be heard. On the same note, you should provide the same emotional safety to your partner. If you want to change something about that person, or if they go into a relationship hoping to change you, you will never create a mutually accepting relationship. Be honest on this point. Once you are married, the flaws of your partner will increase for certain as he/she grows comfortable in the relationship. You have to ask yourself if you want to change something about the person. If you do, you need to look elsewhere. Be accepting and expect the other person to be equally accepting of your flaws. Trying to 'improve' each other will only drive you apart.

You should be committed to becoming a better person, and so should your potential mate. In your relationship with the Father, becoming more Christ-like truly should be your primary goal. Is he/she driven to be a better person? You and your potential mate should strive to do good and always be looking to do the right thing. For both of you, this should be a serious endeavor. A person who seeks to be better is a sensitive and refined person at heart. That means he/she should not be materialistic. Materialistic people tend to not make self-improvement a real priority, and will put personal comfort ahead of doing the right thing.

Your potential mate should treat others with kindness and respect. A person who does not show respect and kindness to others will usually deny you those things eventually. The ability to give is fundamental to long term relationships. Those who are self-absorbed lack this skill and will treat your needs as secondary to their own. Ask yourself some hard questions. Does he/she treat people who are there to serve him/her with respect? Does he/she treat waiters and taxi cab drivers with genuine respect. They should treat people they don't have to be nice to in a kind way. Does he/she treat the people they work with in a respectful way? How does he/she treat family? How people treats their family says a lot about the type of people they are. If he/she treats parents or siblings with a lack of respect, eventually, you will be treated the same way. Gratitude of the heart is a must have character trait. People who cannot appreciate their parents (even the not so good parents) won't know how to give you respect in the end. Gossipers and people who talk bad of family behind their backs shows lack love in their hearts.

The main thing that inspires us to love our Father is His acceptance of who we are. His acceptance and forgiveness drives our relationship with Him. We can call on Him at any time and talk to Him about any thing. In our human relationships, we should expect the same thing. A marriage should be an emotionally safe place built with someone who understands this simple truth. When we feel free to express ourselves, we are freed to grow closer to Father and closer to one another. Father does not mock us or belittle us for our mistakes. He accepts us and works with us to be better. Don't let your feelings lead you before you know where you will be led. Father's plan for you is to be led by your character and not by your emotions. The relationship between a man and a woman must be grounded in true character, or eventually the family will fall. Who you are as a single person will largely determine the kind of person you will become as a married person. Weak people form weak marriages. Weak marriages create weak families.

Sex And The Single Life

Premarital sex is not harmless and it is not something that people must do because they need sex. Premarital sex is a sign of insecurity. In some cases, it is a way of 'taking possession' of a partner with the belief that if sex is offered, the relationship is more certain and stronger. When a woman sleeps with multiple partners, our society recognizes that there may be issues with self-esteem and insecurity. Men, on the other hand, are viewed by the same society as dominant and more masculine for seeking sex with multiple partners. Their peers often praise them for their conquests. But, the truth is that a man who seeks sex with multiple partners is every bit as insecure as the woman doing the same thing. Insecure men are driven to bed as many women as possible to lift their self-esteem. Insecure women need to feel desired as a substitution for real love. Building a strong marriage is already hard enough. Adding issues over one's sexual history makes that task even harder. Anything that you would not be willing to share with a potential mate should generally be avoided.

Why would I discuss this with those who consider themselves to be Christian? Because Christians are engaging in this behavior as much as the general population. It is so common that most people don't really consider it an issue. They see the Christian position as best, but not required. Sex is an assumed part of a man/woman relationship. Society has successfully convinced the general population that sex is a need that cannot be controlled and need not be controlled. Sex has become the 'acceptable Christian weakness'. Christians listen to the so called medical experts that tell us that everyone needs a healthy sex life before marriage.

Experts and science are subject to the political will of the people. When slavery was the political goal of the mainstream, 'science' offered proof that blacks were less than human, and so, not entitled to human rights and protection of law. The desire to escape slavery was 'scientifically' classified as a mental illness and there was a prescribed treatment. There were studies that 'proved' that the black people did not have the capacity to make important political decisions. Science is largely based on faith. Science education does not start with conducting direct experiments to prove everything taught in a textbook. Instead, science education starts with students accepting the witness and conclusions of those who wrote the textbook. We are asked to have faith that the experiments done by others actually happened and that we would reach the conclusions we are offered as facts. If I were a slave owner in America, I would be able to go to church and sleep comfortably in the knowledge that science 'proved' that my brutal treatment of slaves as no more wrong that whipping a horse and slandering a pig. Science would have 'proven' to me that my slaves actually needed to be treated this way.

Science today offers the same comfort to those who need to calm their consciences. For all of human history, a baby was considered a human being from the moment the woman became pregnant. Unfortunately, the sexual revolution made having babies a liability. Science came to the rescue. Science told us that an unborn baby who could not live outside the woman was not really a person. Because that unborn baby was not 'viable' as a person, science told us that it is ok to kill that baby for personal convenience. Diplomatically, they focused on a woman's right to control her own body, rather than a baby's right to the life their behavior (sex) gave the child.

The Father is very clear on whether or not an unborn child is a person. Moses prescribes laws that punish a person who harms a pregnant woman and the baby alone dies. The prophet Jeremiah records that he was called before he was born. The soul enters when there is life inside a woman's body, and not only when the baby becomes 'viable'. 'New' science had to be created to support the killing of children to take away responsibility for the sex act. It is a form of science hypocrisy. Science understands that sex is primarily for procreation. Ninety five percent of marriages give birth to children. The bonding of a man and a woman promotes the best environment to support the resulting offspring. Then science worked to release men and women from the natural consequence of sex, promoting sex as entertainment and not a critical part of human pair bonding.

If you want to talk science, humans have a very long maturation period for their offspring that is far more resource intensive than any other species. Our early life is biologically devoted to mental development over physical development. Only after the mind reaches a certain level of maturity does 'nature' trigger puberty to prepare the body for sex and reproduction. In addition to all of the physical changes, the young mind changes to drive a social structure to facilitate pair bonding. All of this takes more than a decade and a half! The children who enjoy the resources of both parents do far better than single parents. In fact, the number one cause of child poverty is single parenting. It requires two people to bring children to mental, physical, and spiritual maturity. Despite these facts, science and society sell the lie that one parent is sufficient and that men and women don't really need each other.

Organic sex has consequences, but it seems we want our food to be more pure than our relationships. If we take away technology, sex is a different thing. If we take away technology, sex is a tool for permanent, committed relationships. Technology has made it possible for the consequences of sex to be avoided. The Father for good reasons put those consequences there. In Christ, there is balance. Without Christ, sex becomes destructive. Sex in a committed relationship offers spiritual and biological benefits to reinforce the bond between a man and a woman.

The emotional impact of sex is destructive when used in the wrong way. It leaves hearts wounded and trust broken. But, the emotional impact of sex done the Father's way is powerful and helps create the family bonds that support each generation. Instead, technology has made it possible for adults to act like impulsive children with some very dangerous weapons. Technology sells a lie that it is protecting children from being born to unwanting parents by stopping them from being born. Technology sells the idea that we are doing a child a favor to deny him/her life because sex was used for entertainment and to improve self-esteem. In our Father's world, organic sex enables a man and a woman who are entered into a permanent pair bond to extend their bond with children and give a higher calling to their relationship. Science has a place, but faith in our Father should exceed faith in our science when it comes to human relationships.

Family starts with a man or woman learning how to live as one person. Most people are driven to find a mate. By the time a person hits their teenage years, their minds become reoriented to find a mate. Few people start out trying to take as many mates as possible. Such urges are the result of low self-esteem and these urges fail because true self-esteem can only be found by developing righteous character.

Lets us all be honest. Every body started out wanting what God wants for them. Father wants you to know your worth because He knows your worth. Every body wants to be accepted and loved. Everybody struggles when they don't find acceptance and love. Everybody loves the idea of a 'soul mate', that one person who is your perfect match. We all want to feel emotionally safe with at least one person. When that does not happen, we become twisted. In a desperate effort to feel 'ok' about life, we take Father's tools and use them in ways never intended. This is true regardless of your religious belief, culture, country or church affiliation.

Family starts with a man and a woman forming a bond. If the family is to survive and be strong, we have to start with the single man and single woman to prepare them for what lies ahead.

Chapter Eight

The Revelare

What is being asked is that you exchange your religions for a relationship. You are being asked to give up your God and exchange Him for a Father. Abandon your churches and exchange them for an extended family. Live and do all things according to Christ's example by living a life of action over a life of endless contemplation. Jesus came to replace man's religions with participation in a divine family, led by our Father in Heaven. He never intended to replace one set of rituals with another set of rituals. He did not seek to replace one religion with another religion. The very idea of religion removes God as Father, and fellow believers as brothers and sisters.

Jesus came to clear away the dust so that we could see his Father as he sees his Father. Father is with us every minute of every day. He sees us and listens to us every minute of every day. Yet, He is the one person in the room being ignored. Every now and then, we look up to address him and then we go back to ignoring His presence. We wake and say a prayer, and when we leave our bedroom, He is still walking with us. On the drive to work or school, He is with us. When we break for lunch and all the time in between, Father is still with us. We can and should make a point of talking to Him throughout the day. We should be in constant communication with our Father, and not just focus on appointed times. This is what we call a relationship. Religion is when we set aside certain times to pray and then go back to ignoring Him. We would never think to treat another human that way. We would never read answers to a spouse or to a child. We would never spend the day ignoring a person who walks right beside us, pausing every now and then for formal communication and then going back to ignoring him/her. We would never do this because we look at people as real and God as some distant idea. Yes, we may have a form of love, but in the end, we have separated God our Father into a distant entity. Father is so close to you every moment that if He were a man, He would cast his shadow on you every moment. The attitude of God in religion must change. If we accept Him as Father, we should treat Him as Father and as a person.

He is there. Our task is to make ourselves aware that He is there. Many people find this troubling. Some because they don't like knowing that the Father sees all that they do. It can be uncomfortable to tell a new lie knowing that your Father is beside you listening. At some point in time, we all like to bury our heads in the sand and pretend that Father does not see. But, being aware of our Father's presence is also a powerful instrument of change because it means realizing that our secrets are not secrets at all. Knowing that Father is with us can give us the power to change and the strength to stand up for what is right when we feel pressured to do what is wrong. Love the Lord with all your heart, soul, and strength. As you make yourself aware of His ever-present Spirit, you will be transformed.

Love Yourself and Your Neighbor

And love your neighbor as yourself. You cannot really love anyone more than you love yourself. You feed yourself and care for your physical needs. Even when you do what is wrong and disobey what Father asks of you, you are attempting to love yourself. People have a very difficult time feeling bad about themselves so they act out in ways to make themselves feel better. When we cover things with lies, it is an attempt to love oneself by avoiding embarrassment or the judgment of others. Even when we hurt others, we are trying to love ourselves by trying to do something to feel better about ourselves regardless of the outcome. We find balance when we do to others the things we want done to us.

The command to do to others, as we want done to us is a positive command. Jesus did not teach us to simply avoid harming others. What he taught was that we think of the good we want done to ourselves and then do those things to others. This is a very powerful command. It goes beyond 'do no harm' and leads us to doing good. All love starts with self-love. We learn this from our parents during the time in our lives when we are most helpless. Because of the undeserved care we receive as children, in a healthy life, our love circle grows. That love circle is really about self... MY parents... MY friends... MY family. As we grow in love, we claim more and more people as part of ourselves. Jesus teaches that all explicit commands in the Bible share this the underlying principle. We are judged by the same standards that we judge others. We are judged when we fail to treat others as we would want to be treated in that situation.

We all want others to be truthful with us. We invite judgment when we fail to be truthful to others. We want others to treat us with respect. We are judged when we don't treat others with respect. We want others to express and show love. We are judged when we fail to show love. We don't want to be harmed in anyway, so we are judged when we harm others. Father requires that we be mindful of this in everything we do. Isn't this much easier than memorizing hundreds of scriptures?

Practice Kindness

Christians have abandoned the practice of kindness in their personal lives. I told a pastor friend that I always give money or food to anyone who asks me on the streets. His face looked hesitant. He asked me how did I know if the person was in real need and not a drunk looking for drinking money. I told him that Jesus said to feed the hungry, clothe the naked, and give shelter to those who asked. If I deny kindness because I want people to prove their need, then I am responsible to the Father for denying that kindness. I am the one who carries the judgment. But, if I obey my Father and give, then the people receiving my kindness are subject to the Father's judgment if the request is a fraud, and not I. He says that if someone steals from me, give him or her more. He never tells me to evaluate their need. He taught me to show kindness. It is your kindness that might make a person change.

I had a good day some years ago and was given a rather large bonus. On my way home, I saw a homeless man by the train station and I gave him a $100 bill. When this man saw the bill, he chased me down the street to give it back and tell me that he did not deserve such kindness. I told him that my Father says that he need not deserve it, but would receive it because my Father loves him. I remember his gratitude and tears. Whenever I walked past a homeless person, I made sure that each day I left enough for a meal for each person whom I crossed begging on the streets. I generously tip bad servers in restaurants because I don't know that person's struggles and why they may be in a mood that day. I have always been met with overwhelming gratitude. These are my treasures. My Father sees me. At this point in my life, I am compelled to give what I can, when I can. If I suspect a fraud, I tell the person that I am doing this because my Father asked me to, and that if it is misused, it is he/she who will face my Father's judgment. Denying kindness based on some criteria is what the religious do. Practicing kindness is the practice of Father's children. When you go about your day, give to those who ask. Feed the hungry. Do good. Be kind.

Kindness should be the witness of all Christians. It should extend to your family, friends, and to strangers. I remember as a child hearing my parents argue. My sweet mother would go to the kitchen and begin to prepare a snack or meal for my dad as they disagreed. She was committed to being kind to my dad even when tempers were hot. I never forgot that example. Her actions changed the tone of the argument and her kindness put my dad's demeanor in a better place. She never denied him kindness because she disagreed with him. In fact, she became more kind. If you give kindness only to those you feel deserve it, how are you any better than an evil man? Even the evil are kind to their own.

Jesus said that our Father wants mercy and not sacrifice. He taught that Father wants us to be kind and not religious. It is better for a church building to fall apart then to deny kindness to those in need. We are taught by the religious traditionalist to put buildings and budgets before people in need. If your neighborhood is run down and dirty, gather your church and clean the streets of trash. Cut the overgrown lawns of your neighbors. Serve them. Your kindness shows them a glimpse of the Father. Rather than inviting them to a 'service', invite them to a meal. Talk with them and discover what they have to say. Accept them and teach them Father's acceptance. There is a time for preaching and a time for teaching. But kindness is something that should always be practiced. Win over people by your kindness and caring. Show them what the

Father is like by doing what the Father does. He sends rain to the just and the unjust. You too should practice the same. Love covers a multitude of sins.

Be Forgiving

When we enter into a relationship with the Father, he clears away the obstacles to that relationship by not holding past transgressions against us. But, that initial forgiveness is just that - initial forgiveness. To be forgiven in the future comes with conditions. If you fail to extend the same kind of forgiveness to others that Father extended to you, then Father will not forgive you. Jesus taught us to pray, "...forgive us as we forgive others". If you don't forgive others, you will not be forgiven your faults. If we do to others what we want done to us, then forgiveness comes easier. Would you want to be forgiven? Of course you would. So, forgive any and all things done to you. This is the way of our Father. It too must be our way. At the end of the day, I always think of this truth. I always recount the mistakes that I have made and remind myself that I do not have the right to hold another in offense.

Your goal should always be to reflect Heaven on Earth. So many of us imagine that Heaven will be so much better, and if we can just get through those gates, then we will be truly good. But Jesus taught us to pray that God's will be done on Earth as it is in Heaven. The kingdom of Heaven is within you. It is not a place where all things are made whole, but rather Heaven is a place where the whole are gathered to share in our Father's love. Each of us has a responsibility to create Heaven on Earth. We do this by changing who we are while we are here. We change in *this* life.

Reject Religious Traditionalism

Religious traditionalism teaches that salvation is achieved through magic. We say the right words and we are accepted into His Kingdom. It teaches a false doctrine that because we can never deserve mercy that Father just hands it out for free. This is a false teaching. A repentant murderer does not continue to kill. A repentance thief does not continue to steal. A repentant liar does not continue to lie. The works themselves are not the reason we find peace with the Father. The change in our thinking is why we find peace with the Father. Changed actions are the things we want to do because our minds have changed. This is the reason we find peace with the Father. Works are a refection of the heart. Without works, the heart has not changed.

Jesus teaches that when we accept him, we gain a place in Heaven. To accept Jesus is to accept his example. To accept Jesus is to accept the example of his life. To trust in his name does not mean to literally trust in a spoken name. It means to trust in the reputation of that name. We understand this when talking about people. When we do something in a person's name, we do it in the spirit of what that person's life meant or represented. The same is true of the Christ. Belief in his name means we accept the life he lived and take that life as an example of the changes we must make in ourselves. Righteousness by definition is the habit of doing right actions based on right thinking. There are no exceptions to this. The Father's gift is free, but comes with a condition. The condition is to change what you think, and from this changed thinking, to change what you do.

I believe in gravity. I have never jumped from a tall building even though I have no proof that it would kill me. I don't have any personal experience of a person jumping from a tall building. I don't 'know' it will kill me, but I believe it will. That belief controls my actions. That belief is so strong that I would never make such a jump. My belief is so strong that I am convinced it would kill me. I take gravity on faith. True faith changes the way we act. True faith changes what we do in our daily lives. True faith in the Father demands that we listen, trust, and obey.

Abandon religion in favor of true faith. Abandon religion in favor of living a life of true belief. Abandon your religious traditions in favor of common sense. Singing in a church choir is not an expression of faith. Sitting in a pew is not an expression of faith. Paying your respects to God is not an expression of faith. Loving the Lord with all of your heart and then loving your neighbor as yourself is the true and only expression of faith. This is the only path to Heaven.

CPSIA information can be obtained
at www.ICGtesting.com
Printed in the USA
BVHW072044260921
617555BV00002B/148

9 781538 003145